BEAUTY PAYS

DANIEL S. HAMERMESH

BEAUTY PAYS

Why Attractive People Are More Successful

PRINCETON UNIVERSITY PRESS

PRINCETON & OXFORD

Published by Princeton University Press, 41
William Street, Princeton, New Jersey 08540
In the United Kingdom: Princeton University
Press, 6 Oxford Street, Woodstock, Oxfordshire
OX20 1TW
press.princeton.edu

Library of Congress Cataloging-in-Publication
Data

Hamermesh, Daniel S.
    Beauty pays : why attractive people are more
successful / Daniel S. Hamermesh.
        p. cm.
    Includes bibliographical references and index.
    ISBN 978-0-691-14046-9 (hardcover)
    1. Success in business. 2. Success. 3. Beauty,
Personal. I. Title.
    HF5386.H243 2010
    650.1—dc22

                                    2011013548

British Library Cataloging-in-Publication Data
is available

This book has been composed in Bauer Bodoni
and Garamond Premier Pro
Printed on acid-free paper. ∞
Printed in the United States of America
10 9 8 7 6 5 4 3 2 1

CONTENTS

PREFACE

I got involved in studying the economics of beauty in a curious way. Early in 1993, I noticed that the data I was using on another research project included interviewers' ratings of the beauty of the survey's respondents. I thought it would be fun to think about how beauty affects earnings and labor markets generally. The result was the first of the six refereed scholarly papers that I have published on this topic. A serious difficulty for me in this line of research has been that many economists find work on this topic, and even this kind of topic, to be beyond the scope of economic research. That kind of narrow-mindedness has conspired in the past to make economics appear boring in the eyes of many non-economists. As the work of Gary Becker, Steve Levitt, and, to a much lesser extent, my own has shown, economic research can be anything but boring. Many of the topics that we work on, and on which serious economic thinking can shed light, are fun and involve issues that could not be understood using the methods of any other scholarly discipline.

I began working nearly twenty years ago to discover what economics has to say on the topic of physical appearance. Many of the themes that are discussed in this book were first tested out in scholarly papers, and later became part of an ever-evolving lecture that I have delivered in various venues, entitled "The Economics of Beauty." In developing the scholarly papers and in presenting the public lecture, I have received numerous comments from listeners, both other economists and the smart people who happened to show up to hear me. Large numbers of the comments have been useful; and even where they have not been, they have still been fun to receive. Perhaps the most amusing was a comment from a distinguished economist who asked, "Are you sure that beauty isn't just correlated with early-birdness [a term whose meaning was initially completely opaque to me and most of the audience, but presumably alludes to early birds catching worms]?"

I was not the first to look at the relationship between beauty and economic outcomes—that's an old topic. I was, however, the first to examine it using a nationally representative sample of adults, and to do so in the context of economic models of the determination of earnings. My subsequent work broadened this approach into a research agenda that inquired into the "Why?" of this relationship and, more generally, into the meaning of discrimination as perhaps represented by the economic roles of beauty and ugliness. As one former student of mine put it, all of this has led to the development of a subfield that one might dub pulchronomics.

Many of my colleagues have contributed indirectly to this book. The most important have been the coauthors who have worked on beauty topics with me, including the students Ciska Bosman and Amy Parker, and my friends Xin Meng and Junsen Zhang. Crucial throughout have been Jeff Biddle and Gerard

Pfann, who have become the most frequent coauthors in my now forty-three-year professional career. Seminar attendees at a very large number of universities, and especially at the National Bureau of Economic Research Labor Studies meetings, have made comments that have improved some of the papers I discuss in this volume. My labor economist colleagues Gerald Oettinger and Steve Trejo were also very generous with their time to listen to my ideas, as was Melinda Moore.

The authors of all the economic studies that have been published since the early 1990s have also, without intending it, contributed substantially to the work. Three reviewers of an earlier draft of the manuscript made cogent comments that greatly improved the presentation. Particular contributions to the book were also made by Judith Langlois, Vice Provost at the University of Texas at Austin, and probably the leading expert on the perception of beauty by infants. My law professor brother made helpful comments on chapter 8, and at age ninety-one, my late mother, Madeline Hamermesh, solved my search for a good title. Her contribution is the first thing that the reader sees.

Using the 5 to 1 scale that I discuss in chapter 2, I am a 3. In my eyes, my wife of forty-four years, Frances W. Hamermesh, is a 5. (I did, however, make the mistake of commenting in a widely circulated newspaper interview that she was not Isabella Rossellini, nor was I Alec Baldwin.) She has encouraged my work on this topic over nearly two decades. Still more important, she made it clear when it was time to stop producing new work and make the entire oeuvre accessible outside the narrow economics specialty. Her comments on all drafts of the manuscript improved it tremendously. I dedicate this book to this amazing woman:

She walks in beauty, like the night
Of cloudless climes and starry skies:
And all that's best of dark and bright
Meet in her aspect and her eyes:

The smiles that win, the tints that glow,
But tell of days in goodness spent,
A mind at peace with all below,
A heart whose love is innocent!

"She Walks in Beauty," George Gordon, Lord Byron

Daniel S. Hamermesh, Austin, Texas   November 2010

PART I

Background to Beauty

CHAPTER 1

The *Economics* of Beauty

Modern man is obsessed with beauty. From the day we are old enough to recognize our faces in a mirror until well after senility sets in, we are concerned with our looks. A six-year-old girl wants to have clothes like those of her "princess" dolls; a pre-teenage boy may insist on a haircut in the latest style (just as I insisted on my crew cut in 1955); twenty-somethings primp at length before a Saturday night out. Even after our looks, self-presentation, and other characteristics have landed us a mate, we still devote time and money to dyeing our hair, obtaining hair transplants, using cosmetics, obtaining pedicures and manicures, and dressing in the clothes that we spent substantial amounts of time shopping for and eventually buying. Most days we carefully select the right outfits from our wardrobes and groom ourselves thoroughly.

The average American husband spends thirty-two minutes on a typical day washing, dressing, and grooming, while the average American wife spends forty-four minutes. There is no age limit for vanity: Among single American women age seventy and older, for some of whom you might think that physical limitations would reduce the possibility of spending time on grooming, we find forty-three minutes devoted to this activity on a typical day.[1] Many assisted living facilities and nursing homes even offer on-site beauty salons. For most Americans, grooming is an activity in which they are willing to invest substantial chunks of their time.

We not only spend time enhancing our appearance—we spend large sums of money on it too. In 2008, the average American household spent $718 on women's and girls' clothing; $427 on men's and boys' clothing; $655 on infants' clothing, footwear, and other apparel products and services; and $616 on personal care products and services.[2] Such spending totaled roughly $400 billion and accounted for nearly 5 percent of all consumer spending that year. No doubt some of this spending is necessary just to avoid giving olfactory or visual offense to family members, friends, and others whom we meet; but that minimal amount is far less than we actually spend on these items.

There is nothing uniquely modern or American about concerns about dress and personal beautification. Archaeological sites from 2500 BCE Egypt yield evidence of jewelry and other body decoration, and traces of ochre and other body paints are readily available even earlier, from Paleolithic sites in southern France. People in other industrialized countries early in the twenty-first century show similar concerns for their appearance and beauty: For example, in 2001 German husbands spent thirty-nine minutes grooming and dressing, while German wives spent forty-two minutes in these activities, quite close to the American averages. This similarity is remarkable, since you would think that cultural differences might lead to different outcomes.[3] It suggests the universality of concerns about beauty and its effects on human behavior.

The public's responses to beauty today are fairly similar across the world. The Chinese producers of the 2008 Summer Olympics must have believed this when they put an extremely cute nine-year-old girl on worldwide television to lip-sync the singing of a less attractive child who had a better voice.[4] The same attitudes underlay the worldwide brouhaha about the amateur English singer, Susan Boyle, whose contrasting beautiful voice and plain looks generated immense media attention in 2009.

Our preoccupation with looks has fostered the growth of industries devoted to indulging this fascination. Popular books have tried to explain the biological basis for this behavior or to exhort people to grow out of what is viewed as an outdated concern for something that should no longer be relevant for purely biological purposes.[5] Newsstands in every country are cluttered with magazines targeting people of different ages, gender, and sexual preference, counseling their readers on methods to improve their looks. A typical example from the cover of a lifestyle magazine for women offers advice on "Beauty Secrets of the Season." One of its counterparts counsels men on how to "Get Fit, Strong and Lean in 6 Weeks."[6]

The importance of beauty is evident in the results of a telephone survey in the United States.[7] Among the randomly selected people who responded to the survey, more felt that discrimination based on looks in the United States exceeded discrimination on ethnicity/national background than vice-versa. Slightly more people also reported themselves as having experienced discrimination based on their appearance than reported discrimination based on their ethnicity. Average Americans believe that disadvantages based on looks are real and even that they have personally suffered from them.

All well and good—the time and money that we spend on it should enhance our interest in beauty and its effects, and we are worried about and experience negative feelings if our looks are subpar. But is the concern of economists more than just a prurient one in response to this intriguing topic? Part of the answer to this question stems from the nature of economics as a discipline. A very appealing characterization is that economics is the study of scarcity and of the incentives for behavior that scarcity creates. A prerequisite for studying beauty as an economic issue must be that beauty is scarce. For beauty to be scarce, as buyers of goods and renters of workers' time people must enjoy beauty. If they cannot find sufficient beauty supplied freely, and are therefore willing to offer money to obtain more of it, it must be that beauty is scarce.

Take as given the notion that the scarcity of beauty arises from genetic differences in people's looks, so that by some socially determined criteria some people are viewed as better-looking than others. (I discuss what I mean operationally by "beauty" in the next chapter.) Would beauty still be scarce if we were all genetically identical? Of course, this eventuality is not about to occur, but even under this unrealistic scenario it would still make sense to talk about an economics of beauty. So long as people desire to distinguish themselves from others, some of these hypothetical clones will spend more on their appearance than others in order to stand out from the crowd. Some of Dr. Seuss's *Sneetches*—a tribe of birdlike creatures who look identical—illustrate this desire for distinction along one dimension in the face of boring sameness along all others by putting stars on their bellies. The term "scarce beauty" is redundant—by its nature, beauty is scarce.

The other part of the answer to this question stems from what I will demonstrate are the large number of economic outcomes related to beauty—areas where differences in individuals' beauty can directly influence economic behavior. Markets for labor of a variety of types, perhaps even all labor markets, might generate premium pay for good looks and pay penalties for bad looks. The measurement of pay premia and penalties in different jobs and for people belonging to different demographic groups is a standard exercise among economic researchers. Doing so in the case of beauty is a straightforward application.

With every effect on the price of a good or service, in these cases wage rates, which are the prices of workers' time, there is an effect on quantity. How a personal characteristic alters the distribution of workers across jobs and occupations is standard fodder for economists; and beauty is surely a personal characteristic that can change the kinds of jobs and occupations that people choose.

If beauty affects behavior in labor markets and generates differences in wages and the kinds of jobs that we hold, it may also produce changes in how we choose to use our time outside our jobs. How we spend our time at home is not independent of how we spend our time at work or of the kinds of occupations we choose. If differences in beauty alter outcomes in the workplace, they are likely to alter outcomes at home too.

A characteristic like beauty that affects wages and employment will also affect the bottom line of companies and governments that employ the workers whose looks differ. Are certain industries likely to be more significantly affected? How does the existence of concerns about beauty affect companies' sales and profitability? How is executives' pay affected by their beauty?

Perhaps most important, how can companies survive if beauty
is scarce and thus adds to companies' costs and presumably re-
duces their profitability?

The more basic question is why these direct effects on labor-
market outcomes arise. Whose behavior generates the outcomes
that we hope to measure? Aside from allowing us to measure the
importance of the phenomenon of beauty in economic behavior, economics as a policy art/science should be able to isolate
the mechanisms by which it affects outcomes. It is crucial to
know how beauty generates its effects if we are to guard against
giving undue importance to its role in the functioning of labor
markets. It is also important in weighing the benefits and costs
to society of our attitudes about human beauty.

All of these possible economic influences of beauty are direct and are at least potentially measurable. And those measurements can readily be made in monetary terms, or at least
converted into monetary equivalents, so that we can obtain
some feel for the size of the impacts relative to those of other
economic outcomes. Because of the scarcity of beauty, its effects outside markets for labor and goods can also be studied in
economic terms. Marriage is just such a market, although husbands and wives are not bought or sold in rich countries today.
Yet the attributes that we bring to the marriage market affect
the outcomes we obtain in that market, specifically the characteristics of the partner who we match with. Beauty is one of
those attributes, so it is reasonable to assume that differences
in the beauty that we bring to the marriage market will create differences in what we get out of it. We trade our looks for
other things when we date and marry; but what are those
other things, and how much of them do our looks enable us to
acquire?

Taking all of this together, the economic approach treats beauty as scarce and tradable. We trade beauty for additional income that enables us to raise our living standards (satisfy our desires for more things) and for non-monetary characteristics of work and interpersonal relations, such as pleasant colleagues, an enjoyable workplace, and so on, that also make us better off. Researchers in other disciplines, particularly social psychology, have generated massive amounts of research on beauty, occasionally touching on economic issues, particularly in marriage markets. But economists have added something special and new to this fascinating topic—a consistent view of exchange and value related to a central human characteristic—beauty.

The economics of beauty illustrates the power of using very simple economic reasoning to understand phenomena that previously have been approached in other ways. That power, the time and money that are spent on beauty worldwide, and human fascination with beauty, are more than sufficient reasons to spend time thinking about beauty from an economic point of view. The economic approach to beauty is a natural complement to economic research on less general topics such as suicide and sumo wrestling, sleep and commercial sex.[8]

I concentrate on economic issues, introducing studies from the psychology and other literatures only where they amplify the economics or contribute essential foundations to understanding the economics of beauty. These other approaches are important; they have provided many insights into human behavior and garnered a lot of media attention. But because they do not rest on a choice-based economic approach, they cannot provide the particular insights that economic thinking does.[9]

The economic approach is broad, but not all-encompassing. Economic analysis cannot explain what makes some personal characteristics attractive and others not—or why the same individual's looks evoke different responses from each different observer. We take the sources of differences in preferences in the same country and at the same time as outside our purview. It does not describe how responses to personal characteristics differ over the centuries or among societies. It treats these too as given. But knowing what human beauty is—what are the attributes that make the typical onlooker view some people as attractive and others as not—is the essential pre-condition for thinking about the economic impacts of beauty. For that reason, the next chapter describes what we know about the determinants of human beauty, a topic that has received a lot of attention from social psychologists and that underlies what economics has to say about the role of beauty.

CHAPTER 2

In the Eye of the Beholder

DEFINITIONS OF BEAUTY

What is human beauty? How does beauty vary by gender, race, and age? Most important, do observers have at least somewhat consistent views of what makes a person beautiful? In order to answer these questions, we first need to attempt to define beauty. One online dictionary offers a definition of beauty that is relevant for our purposes: "The quality or aggregate of qualities in a person or thing that gives pleasure to the senses or pleasurably exalts the mind or spirit."[1] The term "aggregate of qualities in a person" comes close to describing beauty in an economic context; but it still leaves the definition vague for practical purposes—what qualities, what aggregate? "Beauty is in the eye of the beholder," the first stock phrase that comes to your mind when asked about human beauty, suggests that people's opinions about this question of human beauty differ.

For economic purposes the questions are what characteristics make a person beautiful, and do people agree on what these characteristics are and what expressions of them constitute human beauty. You and I may differ in our views about what beauty is. But if our views about human beauty are somewhat similar, and we are typical individuals, then our opinions are valuable representatives of how the general population views beauty. And if we examine how people have viewed beauty over the ages, we can acquire a more sophisticated understanding of what human beauty is and have more informed opinions when we judge people's looks.

Even if people agreed completely on what expressions of various characteristics constitute beauty, we would still need to decide which particular constellation of characteristics should be considered in the definition. Is it hair or hair color? Weight? Height? Physiognomy—just the face? Internal beauty—character and its expression—reversing the popular saying that beauty is only skin deep? Is it generosity? Sympathy? Facial expression? Dress? Combinations of these? To discuss the economic effects of beauty, I want to narrow the focus as much as possible to faces. One might argue that physiognomy represents only a tiny part of human beauty—and that is correct. Nonetheless, physiognomy can be isolated and used as a basis for judgments about human beauty:

> She reminded me of the daughter that I always had wished for. Bright eyes, a mouth ready to laugh, high cheekbones and luxurious shoulder-length brown hair. The photo didn't show if she was short or tall, fat or thin, bent or erect—it was only a passport photo.[2]

Or, as the psychoanalyst Oliver Sacks put it, "it is the face, first and last, that is judged 'beautiful' in an aesthetic sense."[3]

As these quotations suggest, people can and do make judgments about beauty based only on physiognomy. Throughout this book I examine how judgments about this one manifestation of beauty affect behavior.

No doubt standards of beauty do change over time. The Renoir nudes that enthralled the art world from the 1880s through the early twentieth century would not be regarded as great beauties today—while not unattractive, they are probably too *zaftig* for contemporary tastes. On the other hand, late-nineteenth-century observers almost certainly would have regarded today's models on the runways of Parisian haute couture as incipiently consumptive, perhaps a character out of *La Bohème* (just as my late grandmother, born in Europe in 1887, viewed my thin face as suggesting that I am dangerously underweight). Even within a society, standards of facial beauty do change over time. Standards also differ, or at least used to differ, across societies at roughly similar points in time. The gentleman in figure 2.1 is Rudolf Valentino, the Hollywood heartthrob of the 1920s. Most people even today would agree that he was quite beautiful—presumably that was a major underpinning of his success as a movie actor. The gentleman in figure 2.2 also lived in the early twentieth century, but in the Arctic. While his fellows would have agreed that he is beautiful, it is unlikely that his looks would have landed him a Hollywood movie contract.

Within a society at a point in time, including the worldwide society of developed nations, there is substantial agreement on what constitutes human beauty. I asked three women, ages twenty, thirty-five, and sixty-five, who the sexiest men in the world are today. All three included George Clooney in their list.

Figure 2.1. Rudolf Valentino, actor, 1920s. © Bettmann/CORBIS

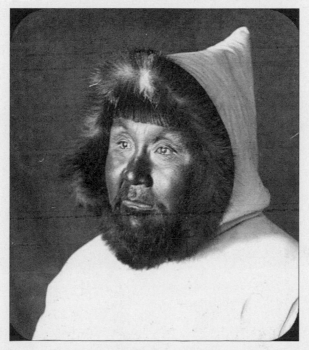

Figure 2.2. Inuit man, 1920s. Photo from Maritime History Archive, Memorial University of Newfoundland, St. John's, NL.

Having presented his picture and those of a number of other men, including Asian and American politicians and actors, to audiences in the United States, Asia, Australia, and Europe, I am certain that there is nearly universal agreement that George Clooney is considered better-looking than almost anyone else.

It is not that George Clooney is a Westerner and there is some kind of universal prejudice in favor of Western faces. Take the two women in figures 2.3 and 2.4. I would wager that most readers, be they Western or not, would consider South

Figure 2.3. Nikki Haley, U.S. politician, 2000s. AP Photo/Alex Brandon, File.

Carolina governor Nikki Haley, who is of South Asian descent, much better-looking than U.S. senator Barbara Mikulski. These cases at least provide anecdotal evidence of the current near-universality of today's standards of human beauty.

Cultural differences do still exist. A recent report on a "fat farm" in Mauritania, one of the poorest countries in the world, illustrates their persistence.[4] This is not the kind of "fat farm" to which rich North Americans retreat to lose weight, but one where young girls are fed, and even force-fed, to produce rotund young adults who are viewed as attractive. But even this unusual cultural difference appears to be diminishing in importance as Mauritania industrializes and becomes more integrated with the outside world.[5]

Figure 2.4. Barbara Mikulski, U.S. politician, 2000s. Official government photo from the U.S. Senate Historical Office.

WHY DO BEAUTY STANDARDS MATTER?

Unless people agree on what constitutes human beauty—unless there is at least a somewhat common standard of beauty—it cannot have any *independent* effect on outcomes such as earnings. It might seem to have an effect, even if people disagreed about beauty, but that could only be if other characteristics that affect those outcomes are related to beauty.

These same arguments apply to the role of beauty in other areas in which human beings trade. We trade our characteristics when we enter into a marriage. As the story of Jacob's efforts to win the hand of Rachel "of beautiful form and fair to look at" illustrates, throughout human history men who can raise more sheep, produce more crops, or earn more dollars in the stock market have used these characteristics to obtain more desirable (and, in some societies and epochs, more) wives.[6] If men agree on feminine beauty, just as in labor markets those women viewed as beautiful will command a higher price, either explicitly or in the form of husbands who can provide them with more resources. They will obtain more and better food, an easier lifestyle, more freedom to do what they want, and other benefits. As men and women become more equal economically, so long as women have common views about men's beauty, the same behavior will apply in reverse: Women who have more to offer men, including the economic advantages they can offer prospective husbands, will obtain the better-looking husbands.

So long as there are common standards of beauty, they will affect outcomes in any market where beauty affects transactions—where it affects what is traded. That is as true for hiring workers as it is for marriage contracts. The question for analyzing the economic effects of beauty is whether the idea of common beauty standards is represented by more than just the pictorial anecdotes presented here. Do people agree, at least to some extent, on which of their fellows are good-looking and which are not? Do they share common views of human beauty?

HOW DO WE MEASURE HUMAN BEAUTY?

We can't see whether there are common standards of beauty unless we are able to compare different people's views about beauty. And we can't easily compare them unless we can somehow measure them. The difficulty is that there is no single way to attach numerical scores to observers' beliefs about the beauty of the people they see. When I was a senior in high school we read Marlowe's *Dr. Faustus*, in which the title character describes a vision of Helen of Troy and declaims, "Is this the face that launch'd a thousand ships, and burnt the topless towers of Ilium?" This prompted one of my fellow nerds to suggest that we should measure the pulchritude of the girls in our class in milli-Helens! This is as reasonable a subjective measuring device as another, but perhaps unsurprisingly it has not been applied in research on beauty.

One might, for example, use a numerical rating scheme and use a 10 to 1 scale. One might instead use a 5 to 1 scale. To see that these are not the same, look at the next five people you see and give each one a rating on a 5 to 1 scale. Ask yourself afterward: "If I had instead used a 10 to 1 scale, would my ratings just have been double those that I gave on the 5 to 1 scale?" I doubt it. In particular, I would bet that scores of 10 on the 10 to 1 scale would be substantially less frequent than the top score on the 5 to 1 scale.

In asking onlookers to rate people's beauty, do we attach verbal descriptions to the numerical ratings that observers are asked to give, or are they simply asked to choose a score? Even with the same scale, say 5 to 1, the answers will differ depending upon what, if anything, the observer is told about the meaning of the scores.

What are the observers asked to rate—people standing in front of them, or pictures? Both approaches have been used, and the difference between them forms the main underlying distinction among studies of beauty. Ratings of the same person by the same observer will differ between the two methods. The picture may show her looking radiant upon her college graduation, or him beaming on his wedding day. People do not react the same way to the camera, and it is impossible to adjust for differences in their reactions when we use observers' ratings of pictures. Some may be dressed well for the picture, others dressed sloppily. Some may be captured scowling, while others have a smile that is glowing enough to turn a 4 into a 5.

Assuming that we rely on ratings of pictures, what are they pictures of? What are the observers asked to rate? Faces alone? Head and shoulders? Full body? Posed or not? Since I have defined beauty for the purpose of this study as physiognomy, head and shoulders, or even the face alone, would be best; but pictures like that are not always available.

The problem is equally, but differently, challenging if we rely on ratings of people who are being interviewed face-to-face. If nothing else, and even with the most explicit instructions, interviewers will tend to base their assessments on the nature of the interactions that they have already had with the person. Does the interviewee answer the door in a dress suit, or in a sweat suit post-workout? Is she at the end of a tiring day, or is she fresh and ready to deal with whatever the world may bring? All of these variations in appearance and behavior will condition how the interviewer assesses her looks.

With both photographs and interviews, it is impossible to be sure that the rater is basing the rating solely on physiognomy. A restriction to physiognomy is more likely with pictures, but even there, weight may enter into the rating (remember the Renoir model). In the end, it is impossible to restrict ratings to be objective—the rating of beauty is inherently subjective. People will always disagree to some extent.

While there may be universal standards of beauty, and thus substantial agreement on what is beautiful, there are no universal standards on how people in different countries and cultures respond when confronted by what appear to be identical requests to rate others' beauty. Even with the best translation, what appear to be the same rating systems may have different meanings in different societies. And there may be international differences in raters' generosity or willingness to make fine distinctions.

There is no way of avoiding these problems. The best we can do in interpreting studies of the effects of beauty is to be sure that raters of beauty were monitored so that they adhered to strict guidelines that are at least internally consistent when they provided their ratings.

The most widely used scale in the beauty literature has been a 5 to 1 rating scheme, usually with instructions to the interviewers/raters about what these ratings mean. The numerical scores were defined in instructions to interviewers in a nationally representative 1971 survey conducted by the University of

Michigan. They have been used with minor variations in many subsequent studies, both those based on observations during live interviews and those based on ratings of photographs.[7]

Near the end of a lengthy interview in the Michigan survey, the interviewer was instructed to "rate the respondent's physical appearance" using the scale:

5   Strikingly handsome or beautiful

4   Good-looking (above average for age and sex)

3   Average looks for age and sex

2   Quite plain (below average for age and sex)

1   Homely

Note the parenthetical qualifiers that were included to induce the interviewers to abstract from preconceptions that they might have about age or gender differences in looks.

To get a feel for the use of this rating scheme, look at the next ten strangers you see and try rating their looks along this scale. Don't intellectualize about your rating—as the interviewers did, it should be a snap response to your impressions. I would be surprised if you cannot easily distinguish a "4" from a "2" among the people you encounter.

I was obsessed by these data in the first few days after I discovered them. I walked around my campus mentally rating the beauty of most of the people I passed on this 5 to 1 scale. I admit that I also rated my colleagues' looks on this scale, thus violating the anonymity that should exist between subject and rater but that is necessarily violated in ratings based on interviews.

The distributions of these interviewers' ratings along the 5 to 1 scale in this study and in a related study conducted later in the 1970s are shown in table 2.1, separately for men and women.

TABLE 2.1
Ratings of Appearance, Quality of American Life, and Quality of Employment
Surveys, Americans Ages 18–64, 1970s (percent distributions)*

	Women	Men
Strikingly handsome or beautiful (5)	3	2
Good-looking (above average for age and sex) (4)	31	27
Average looks for age and sex (3)	51	59
Quite plain (below average for age and sex) (2)	13	11
Homely (1)	2	1

*Tabulations from raw data describing 1,495 women and 1,279 men.

Here, as in many subsequent tabulations of ratings of beauty based on interviews, more individuals are assessed as being in the top two categories than in the bottom two. Interviewers' formal subjective ratings of beauty are not quite characterized by a Lake Wobegon effect—not everyone is above average in beauty—but the average person whose beauty is assessed in this study is considered above average.

Interviewer-based ratings from vastly different cultures produce the same general results. Evidence from a survey in Shanghai, China, from the mid-1990s demonstrates the similarity of ratings to those in the United States. The Chinese interviewers were, though, particularly unwilling to rate people as below-average in looks—only 1 percent of men, and 1 percent of women, were rated as below-average or ugly. Nearly two-thirds of each group was rated as average.

Using the same 5 to 1 scale as in table 2.1, raters examined nearly 2,500 photographs of students who entered a large, prestigious law school between 1969 and 1984. Each photograph (typically head-and-shoulders shots) was rated by four different observers. As with the interview ratings, nearly half the people were rated as average-looking.

The 5 to 1 scale or a minor variant is most common, but others have been used. One study asked six raters (three male and three female undergraduate students) to use a 10 to 1 scale to examine photographs to assess the looks of a group of ninety-four professors (whom the six students did not know).[8] As in the law students' study, there was no tendency to rate the professors' looks as above the middle of the 10-point scale—indeed, more were rated 5 or less than were rated 6 or above. Partly this may be due to the professors' ages (averaging fifty) being so different from those of the undergraduates doing the ratings. Partly it may just be the sample: When asked why his ratings were particularly low, one male student remarked, "Because these profs are really ugly!"

DO OBSERVERS AGREE ON BEAUTY?

That people are biased in favor of judging others' beauty as on average being above-average, or even as below-average, is not a problem—it is easy to adjust statistically for these biases in drawing conclusions about the relationship between differences in beauty and any economic or other outcome. The tougher question is whether people agree on the beauty of a particular individual, and the extent of that agreement, if any. Without that there would be no common standards of beauty. Beauty would have no meaning in an economic context, since its diffuseness would mean it could not be scarce. And I would not be writing this book!

There are two different ways to discover the extent of raters' agreement about people's beauty. The first, which has been used only rarely, is to look at how raters' assessments of people's beauty vary when they view the same individuals at different times. Answers using this approach can be seen from a study based on pictures of economists. I asked four students who were just beginning their graduate studies to rate the looks of a large number of pictures of leading economists, many of whom were included multiple times and submitted a different photograph each time. Of course, the same individual received different ratings for different pictures, but those differences were small compared to the differences in the average ratings received by different economists.[9]

Answers based on interviews can be seen from a nationally representative study undertaken in Canada, in which the same people were interviewed in 1977, 1979, and 1981. Each individual was contacted by a different interviewer in each year, allowing an opportunity for different views of the interviewee's looks to be expressed. The interviewers were asked to assess looks using the 5 to 1 scale. Comparing ratings in adjacent years, 54 percent of women and 54 percent of men were rated identically in each of the two years; and only 3 percent of women and 2 percent of men received a rating in the second year of a pair that differed by more than 1 from the rating that they had received in the first year of that pair.[10] Even in different interactions with different interviewers there was a remarkable tendency to view the interviewees' looks very much the same way.

The second way of testing for consistency in our views of others' beauty is to ask a group of individuals to provide independent ratings of another person's looks. Typically this has been done by showing each of a number of people, none of whom can contact the others, the same photograph. While there will be disagreements, the question is whether they are small, so that the averages inform us about general perceptions of each person's looks.

As an example, take the ratings of the law students' photos described earlier. Complete agreement—all four observers giving the exact same score to a photograph—was fairly uncommon, occurring for only 14 percent of the photos. But near agreement, defined as all four ratings the same, as three of four raters rating the picture identically, or as two pairs of raters who differ by only 1 point on the 5-point scale, occurred with the photos of 67 percent of the female students and 75 percent of the male photos. Only one-tenth of 1 percent of the students were rated differently by all four raters. Complete disagreement about looks is an extraordinarily rare event.

Even in the case of the professors, where the 10 to 1 scale allows for a lot more minor disagreement among the six raters, 54 percent of the professors were rated identically by at least three of the six raters. Among the economists, who were also rated on the 10 to 1 scale, 28 percent of the pictures received the same score from three of the four raters, and 80 percent were rated identically by at least two of the four.

There are consistent differences in how individuals rate each other's beauty. Within the same culture some people are always harsh in rating their fellow citizens' looks, and others are consistently more generous. In the study that established the 5-point rating scheme, each of sixty interviewers rated at least ten subjects. The average ratings ranged from 3.6 (closer to above-average than to average) by the most generous interviewer down to 2.4 (closer to plain than to average) by the most negative interviewer. But only 10 percent of the differences in the ratings of interviewees can be ascribed to judgments by raters who applied particularly harsh or generous standards. While interviewers do have different standards, the effects of their differences are dwarfed by the inherent differences in people's looks.[11]

About half of the interviewers in that study were between ages twenty-two and forty-nine, the other half were between ages fifty and seventy-four. Despite their possibly different perspectives on the subjects' looks, there were no statistically meaningful differences in the ratings given by interviewers of different ages. But while interviewers' age was independent of the ratings that they assigned, there were differences by gender. Men seemed to be stingier raters of the subjects' beauty.

There are also differences across countries, probably having to do with cultural differences in people's willingness to say something negative about their fellows. For instance, Americans seem slightly more willing than their Canadian neighbors to label someone as plain or homely. As noted earlier, in the Shanghainese data, only 1 percent of the interviewees were rated as below average. The only useful distinction in those data is between those rated as average and those rated as pretty or very pretty.

Despite these consistent disagreements and biases, the answer to the titular question of this section is a resounding, "MOSTLY!" There is no universal agreement by groups of people on anyone else's beauty. Some people are harsh judges of others' looks, while other people are generous in their appraisals. But individuals do tend to view others' beauty similarly, although not identically. Someone who is considered above-average in looks by one observer will be viewed the same way by most other observers. Someone who a randomly selected person thinks is quite ugly will be viewed as quite ugly by most other observers. Yes, there are disagreements, but there is also a lot of agreement. There is no unique view about beauty—no unique standard. But because people tend to view human beauty similarly, those who are generally viewed as good-looking possess a characteristic—their beauty—that appeals to most other human beings in similar ways and that *ipso facto* is in short supply. Human beauty is scarce.

DOES BEAUTY DIFFER BY GENDER, RACE, OR AGE? WHAT MAKES YOU BEAUTIFUL?

Are women better-looking than men? I think so when I think romantically, but you no doubt have your own views on this subject. The question, though, is whether we think that way when we try to assess people's looks objectively. The average male in the data underlying table 2.1 was rated almost the same as the average woman. In the Shanghai data, women were rated as slightly better-looking than men, with the difference resulting from more women being rated as beautiful.

This near equality only arises if the individuals being rated are chosen randomly. Women constituted only 12 percent of the law students who entered the prestigious law school between 1969 and 1974. The average rating of their looks was 3.1, compared to the 2.8 average rating of their male fellow students, perhaps because those few women were special in many other ways. By the next decade, female students had increased to 31 percent of the entering classes, and the difference in average looks between male and female students was only half as large as before. Selection into the sample can produce unequal averages of the ratings of the looks of men and women. But where men and women are roughly equally represented among the subjects, the average ratings of men's and women's looks are usually nearly identical.

While average ratings of looks are roughly equal by gender, the distributions differ, as the columns in table 2.1 illustrate. Ratings of women's looks were more extreme than ratings of men's: More were rated as plain or homely, more were rated as strikingly beautiful or above-average, and fewer were rated as possessing average looks. Interviewers react more strongly to women's looks, both positively and negatively in other interview studies too; and in studies examining photographs, women are also viewed more extremely than men. For example, 14 percent of the ratings of female professors were above 7, while only 6 percent of the ratings of male professors were.

Whether beauty differs by race is another concern—if, for example, employers perceive African Americans' beauty differently from that of whites, any differences in earnings related to race could be confounded by disparate treatment based on looks rather on than on race per se. In the two American studies from the 1970s the interviewers, nearly all of whom were white, gave almost identical ratings on average to whites and African Americans. But they did rate subjects of different races differently, reacting more extremely to the whites than to the African Americans. Thirteen percent of whites were rated as plain or homely, while only 10 percent of African Americans were. At the upper end, 32 percent of whites were viewed as being at least above-average, while only 28 percent of African Americans were. There may well be differences between how members of other races—Asian Americans, for example—would be rated by the white raters, but we just have no information on that possibility.

Whether we consider looks by gender or race, we reach the same conclusion. There are no differences in averages, but the distributions of ratings of women's looks are more dispersed than those of men's, and of whites' looks more than those of African Americans.

The same conclusion cannot be drawn about differences in ratings of the beauty of people of different ages. Ratings of women, and of men from studies conducted in the 1970s, demonstrate that the looks of younger people are rated on average more favorably than those of older people. Even though interviewers were explicitly instructed to adjust "for age and sex," they couldn't.

The differences in ratings by age are not small. Of women in the 18–29 group, 45 percent were rated at least above-average, while only 18 percent of women 50–64 were rated that favorably, a remarkable drop-off. The decline in perceived looks with age is smaller among men, with 36 percent of men ages 18–29 rated above-average, while 21 percent of men 50–64 were rated that favorably. Age is harsher on our perceptions of women's looks.

There is nothing unique about the differences in perceived beauty by age in our Western culture. Even in China, where the stereotype is one of great respect for older people, younger people's beauty is rated more positively. The average rating of people ages 22–34 in the Shanghai data was 3.5; that of people ages 35–49 was 3.4, while people 50 and over received ratings that only averaged 3.3.[12] The Chinese observers were no more able to separate beauty from age than their American counterparts.

Why these age differences persist is not a topic for this book—their existence is all that is important, as the correlation of perceived beauty with age dictates that any study of the impact of beauty must adjust for age if we believe that age might also affect the outcome. It is interesting, though, to speculate why these differences arise. It might be that people's inability to adjust mentally for age when they rate others' looks is evolutionarily valuable. We are conditioned to believe that youth and beauty go together, since that belief encourages mating at a time when fecundity is near its maximum.[13]

This evidence on beauty and age does not compare the same people over their lifetimes, and no large-scale study has followed the same people's looks over large parts of their lives. Smaller studies have done this, though, taking pictures of people at an early age and asking raters to rate them and photos of the same people taken much later in life. The ratings were very highly correlated. The general conclusion is, "Ugly ducklings generally blossom into ugly ducks."[14]

What is it about a person's face that leads most observers to view it as good-looking? What characteristics of another person's face cause most of us to consider it plain or even homely? The answers to these questions are not required for our purposes here: So long as people agree about others' looks, and so long as we can adjust for any systematic differences across culture, age, gender, race, or other characteristics in how looks are viewed, we can use observers' common agreements about individuals' looks to analyze the impacts of looks on outcomes and even on success in a variety of areas.

Although not economic, these questions are fascinating; and they have been studied by a number of social psychologists. The leading work, by my University of Texas colleague Judith Langlois, has produced a number of interesting results, among which are: (1) Agreement on what constitutes human beauty, and especially human ugliness, is formed very early in life—probably during infancy. (2) Symmetry is beauty—a symmetric face is considered beautiful, while increasingly asymmetric faces are viewed as increasingly ugly.[15]

CAN WE BECOME MORE BEAUTIFUL?

The evidence makes it clear that people's looks relative to those of others of their age do not change greatly over their lifetimes. But with common agreement on looks, why don't people alter them to meet the commonly agreed-upon standards of beauty of the society where they live? If beauty can pay off, why not become beautiful?

The prospect of becoming better-looking is endlessly appealing to people. But even fiction, such as the movie *Face-Off* with John Travolta, recognizes that greatly changing one's looks is exceedingly difficult. Procedures to remove blemishes and wrinkles are done all the time, as is evidenced by actors, actresses, and politicians who have "had a lot of work done," using the Hollywood terminology. In 2007, Americans received over 4.6 million injections of Botox, had 285,000 nose-reshaping surgeries, and 241,000 eyelid surgeries. All of this was good business for plastic surgeons, to the tune of $12 billion on cosmetic plastic surgery.[16]

Citizens of other wealthy countries are less wedded to these procedures, but they too devote substantial resources to them. In 2006, Britons devoted about $800 million to cosmetic procedures, about one-third as much per capita as Americans, but enough to lead the EU on a per-capita basis. This was four times more than they had spent in 2001. Italians ranked second in Europe in spending on cosmetic surgery, France came third, closely followed by Germany.[17]

While fictional beautification methods may convert "3" or even "1" people into "5's," their real-world counterparts do not and cannot remove the essential asymmetries that detract from how their beauty is perceived by the rest of humankind. The efforts can help, to the extent that perceptions of human beauty are based in characteristics other than the symmetry of facial features. We know that the beauty of younger people is perceived more positively than that of their elders, so that attempting to find surgical fountains of youth will help improve how our beauty is perceived. Nonetheless, these changes are likely to be small.

Perhaps the payoffs to plastic surgery are simply not great enough to justify the spending that might make one substantially more beautiful. Perhaps they are, but the costs of the improvement, both in dollar terms and in pain and suffering, are too large to get people to undergo the surgery. These possibilities are suggested by some results describing examples of plastic surgery in Korea. For most people, the potential economic gains from the improvements in beauty were very far from justifying even the monetary cost of the procedure, much less the psychological cost—the "pain and suffering"—of undergoing any surgery.[18]

If plastic surgery cannot convert us all to beauties, or we cannot afford the cost of surgery, or we don't want to bear the pain of the surgery that would be required to accomplish this, maybe a simpler approach would work: Buy better clothing, use more cosmetics, get better coiffed, etc. Magazines and newspaper columns are devoted to "dressing for success" and "beauty makeovers," including recommendations of the appropriate clothing, hairstyle, manicure, etc. Does this kind of spending really work? Can we make ourselves more beautiful by spending more on non-surgical methods of beauty enhancement?

The Shanghai survey collected information on the amount that each woman spent each month on clothing, cosmetics, and hair care, as well as on her looks, as rated by the interviewer. Comparing the woman who spent the average amount on these items per month, to another who spent nothing, the average woman's spending only raised her looks from 3.31 to 3.36. One might think that these women could do better by spending still more; and it is true that increasing spending to five times the average (over 20 percent of average household income) would raise the rating of the average woman's beauty to 3.56. But the data make it very clear that the extra effect of this spending diminishes the more one has already spent.[19]

Many popular stories suggest that people believe that wardrobe, hairstyle, cosmetics, and surgery will improve their economic outlook.[20] The evidence indicates that this is simply wrong: in the Chinese study each dollar spent on improving beauty brought back only four cents on average. Just as much of our spending on health may not increase our longevity, but may let us enjoy life more, so too it may make sense to spend on plastic surgery and better clothes. The best reason for this kind of spending is that it makes you happier. It is not a good investment if you seek only the narrow goal of economic improvement.

Someday technology may allow us to reach the point where we can improve our beauty easily and without great cost. Right now, though, we are so far away from that point that for most of us the beauty that we have attained as young adults is not going to be greatly altered, compared to the beauty of our contemporaries, by natural changes that occur as we age, nor by any surgical or cosmetic efforts that we undertake to improve it. Barring disfiguring accidents, we are basically stuck with what nature and perhaps early nurture have given us.

THE STAGE IS SET

The array of evidence presented here provides the background for discussing how an economic way of thinking about beauty might proceed—how what we know about human perceptions of human beauty conditions the analysis of beauty's effects. The main consistent results are:

1. Most important of all, there is substantial agreement among observers about what constitutes facial beauty. Beauty is in the eye of the beholder, but most beholders view beauty similarly. Some people are consistently regarded as above-average or even beautiful, while others are generally regarded as plain or even downright homely.
2. In many studies, more people are rated as good- than as bad-looking.
3. Beauty is fleeting—and youth is beauty. Even when we are asked to account for individuals' ages in judging their looks, we just cannot do it. People tend to rate young adults as more attractive than older people.
4. People who are viewed as relatively good-looking when young tend to be rated as relatively good-looking when older.
5. While looks can be altered by clothing, cosmetics, and other short-term investments, the effects of these improvements are minor. Even plastic surgery doesn't make

a huge difference. The old adage, "You can't make a silk purse out of a sow's ear," applies to human looks as well as to porcine purses. Even with today's technology and lower costs, we are generally stuck with what nature has given us in the way of looks.

6. Women's looks are perceived differently from men's—observers are more likely to rate women as beautiful or ugly, and are more likely to disagree about women's looks.

Taking all these considerations together, our agreement on what constitutes beauty allows sufficient scope for beauty to affect behavior in many facets of economic life. Because people agree about others' looks to at least some extent, markets for labor, mates, credit, and no doubt other markets, can be affected in ways that alter how participants in those markets behave and that help to determine the benefits that they obtain.

PART II

Beauty on the Job: What and Why

CHAPTER 3

Beauty and the Worker

THE CENTRAL QUESTIONS

Everybody assumes that better-looking people make more money. But why should that be? Is it even true? And if it is true, how much more do they make? Put simply, how much extra does a good-looking worker earn than an average-looking worker? How much less than an average-looking worker does a bad-looking worker make? These sound like simple questions, but they aren't. Because beauty may be related to other characteristics that workers possess, we need to separate out the effects of beauty on income from those of other things that may be related to both beauty and income. Answers to these questions are the most widely available in the burgeoning literature in pulchronomics—the economics of beauty. We have a pretty good feel today for the general sizes of the beauty premium and the ugliness penalty.

Does beauty affect income differently for men and women? Does it affect income differently among older workers than among younger workers? How about by race or ethnicity? While I concentrate on the United States throughout most of this book, one wonders whether the impacts of beauty on incomes differ between the United States and other countries. Is there a special "hang-up" with beauty in the American labor market that produces unusually large effects on incomes compared to elsewhere? How have gains in income that result from one's beauty changed over time? Are we outgrowing a fixation on looks, or does the effect of looks in labor markets loom even larger?

HOW CAN BEAUTY AFFECT EARNINGS?

Imagine a world with only two companies, each with a single boss who makes all the hiring decisions. Call the bosses Cathy and Deb. Their companies make completely different products—they do not compete with each other in what they sell; and each employs half of the workers in this imaginary world. Both Cathy and Deb like to surround themselves with workers whom they view as beautiful. Doing so makes them feel better and enhances their well-being beyond the tremendous profits they will earn from their workers' efforts. All the workers are equally productive—each has the same set of skills, each can help the employer produce as much as any other worker can. All workers work the same number of hours per year. Half the workers are cloned from one parent, Al; the other half are cloned from another parent, Bob. All Al workers look alike, as do all Bob workers; but an Al worker looks different from a Bob worker.

How much will each Al worker be paid? How much will each Bob worker be paid? We know that each Al worker will earn the same as every other Al worker—they are identical in all respects. The same is true for each of the Bob workers—they too are identical to each other. The only issue is how Al workers' wages will differ from Bob workers' wages.

Because they, like people generally, share common standards of beauty, it's likely that Cathy and Deb think somewhat similarly about the looks of their potential employees. What if both Cathy and Deb think that Al workers are beautiful, while Bob workers are not? If Al and Bob workers were paid the same wage, both Cathy and Deb would want to hire all the Al workers. But there are only enough Al workers for one of them. The only way that competition for the Al workers can assign them to Cathy or Deb is if the wages of Al workers are bid up to the point where their extra pay just offsets the extra satisfaction that the "winning" employer gets from employing the Al workers.

To win the competition for the (good-looking) Al workers, Cathy must pay them a premium, just enough to outbid Deb. Her costs are higher than Deb's, who is stuck with the Bob workers who both Deb and she view as ugly. But Cathy is just as happy about her employees as Deb, since her extra costs are offset by the extra satisfaction she gets from employing the Al workers whom Deb and she both view as beautiful. With a common standard of beauty, labor markets establish premium pay for the good-looking workers—or, viewed in reverse, penalty pay for the ugly workers—based on the extent to which employers value looks. In this case the premium is the amount that Cathy has to pay to overcome Deb's desire for the good-looking Al workers.

This example assumed that Cathy's and Deb's preferences for their workers' beauty determine what wages would be. What if, though, Cathy and Deb don't really care about their workers' looks, but their customers care about the looks of the workers who make the goods they buy, or more realistically, about the looks of the workers who are selling to them? If both Cathy's and Deb's customers prefer Al-type workers, Al-type workers will receive higher wages than Bob-type workers. The outcomes are the same, whether it is Cathy's and Deb's own preferences that determine the effect of looks on wages, or whether their behavior just expresses their customers' preferences.

Whose preferences generate premium pay for beauty, and penalties for ugliness, can't be determined just by showing the existence and size of those differences in earnings—it requires a deeper investigation of underlying causes. We must first see whether and by how much beauty is rewarded, as we do in this chapter. We need to discover how it affects people's choices of what work to undertake; and we need to see how companies' sales and profits relate to their employees' looks.

HOW MUCH MORE DO GOOD-LOOKING PEOPLE MAKE?

To begin answering these questions, take the most important: To what extent does beauty affect the earnings of the typical worker? On its face this seems to be a simple task: Find a large group of individuals, randomly chosen from a country's population; get measures of their looks, by one of the methods we have discussed; obtain information on their earnings; and compare their earnings to their looks.

This is not so easy to do for the United States as one might think or hope—the most recent nationally random data that provide this information are from surveys collected in the

1970s—the data underlying table 2.1. Regrettably, no nationally representative set of data since the 1970s contains information on earnings and also ratings of the respondents' beauty. This means that these effects are best described as what *were* the effects of beauty on earnings. But using these data we can get an initial picture of how beauty and earnings are related in the general population.

Using these large random samples of women and men, we can compare their earnings to the ratings of their looks. Compared to the average group (people rated as 3 on the 5 to 1 scale), below-average looking women (rated 2 or 1 on the scale) earn 3 percent less, while below-average looking men earn 22 percent less. Above-average looking women (rated 4 or 5 on the scale) earn 4 percent more than the average-looking, while above-average looking men earn 3 percent more. There is a premium for good looks, a penalty for bad looks. Except for the penalty for the 11 percent of men whose looks are rated as below-average, these differences in earnings are not large; but they are in the directions that you would expect.

These simple differences are interesting; but are they genuine, or do they merely reflect the strong possibility that beauty and other things that increase one's earnings are related? The number of "other things" is potentially huge; but a thorough approach would take anything that has repeatedly been shown to affect earnings, and would then adjust for its impacts in order to isolate the effect of beauty on earnings. These other factors include:

- Education (increasing earnings)—what if better-looking people are better educated?

- Age (increasing earnings up to some point, perhaps to the mid-fifties for a typical worker, then reducing earnings)—we know that age and beauty are related
- Health (healthier people earn more)—beauty may be related to health
- Union membership (increasing earnings)
- Marital status (positive effects among men, negative effects among women)—beauty may be related to whether you are married or not
- Race/ethnicity (minorities earn less than non-Hispanic whites)
- Size of city (higher earnings in bigger cities and in metropolitan as opposed to non-metropolitan and rural areas)
- Region (higher in the East than in the South)
- Nativity (immigrants earn less than natives)
- Family background (lower among people whose parents were immigrants)
- Size of company (higher in big firms) or plant (higher in larger plants)
- Years with the company (increasing earnings until late in a person's tenure with the company)

Numerous studies have shown that each of these factors affects earnings. Since most or even all of them might differ systematically with an individual's looks, to isolate the effect of looks on earnings we need to adjust earnings using data on as many of them as we can.

Table 3.1 shows the average impacts of beauty combining data from the two samples of Americans in the 1970s. The penalties for below-average looks, and the premia for above-

TABLE 3.1
Percentage Impacts of Looks on Earnings, U.S., 1970s (compared to average-looking workers, rated 3), Adjusted for Many Other Determinants of Earnings

Looks	Women	Men
Above Average (4 or 5)	8*	4
Below Average (2 or 1)	−4*	−13*

*Denotes statistically different from zero. Reproduced from Daniel Hamermesh and Jeff Biddle, "Beauty and the Labor Market," *American Economic Review* 84 (December 1994), pp. 1174–94.

average looks, are based on statistical analyses that adjusted earnings for most of these other factors in order to isolate the effect of differences in beauty. An asterisk (*) denotes that the impact is statistically meaningful—that we can be fairly sure that looks have some effect on earnings.

Note that these numbers are in the same directions as the numbers that did not account for all the other determinants of earnings. They do change—these other determinants of earnings do matter; but the basic conclusion, that there is a penalty to earnings for bad looks and premium pay for good looks, is unaltered. If asked, "What is the overall effect of looks on earnings in the U.S.?" the best answer, based on table 3.1, is that the bottom 15 percent of women by looks, those rated as below-average (2 or 1), received 4 percent lower pay than average-looking women. The top one-third of women by looks, those rated as above-average (4 or 5), received 8 percent more than average-lookers. For men, the comparable figures are a 13 percent penalty and a 4 percent premium.

There is nothing written in stone about these numbers. No doubt, if other nationally representative data were available, the estimates of these effects would differ. But we can be fairly sure that the effects of beauty on earnings are in the ballpark of the figures in table 3.1.

These numbers mean little by themselves without comparisons to the effects of other determinants of differences in earnings. How does the 17 percent excess of good-looking men's earnings over those of bad-looking men's (13 percent penalty plus 4 percent premium) compare to the effects of differences in other characteristics on men's earnings? How does the 12 percent shortfall of plain or homely women's earnings from above-average or beautiful women's (4 percent penalty plus 8 percent premium) compare to other effects on women's earnings?

By far the most thoroughly examined determinant of earnings is education. A good estimate for the United States today is that each additional year of schooling raises the earnings of otherwise identical workers by around 10 percent.[1] This effect is a bit more than that of women's good looks; and it implies that men's good looks have an impact on their earnings at least as large as an additional one-and-a-half years of school.

Among the other factors that affect earnings are work experience and whether a workplace is unionized. For a forty-year-old man the impact of good looks on earnings is about the same as that of an additional five years of work experience, and also about the same as that of working in a unionized workplace.[2] The effects of beauty on earnings are not immense, but they are certainly substantial.

When viewed in the context of an entire working life, they seem even larger. In 2010, the average worker earned about $20 per hour. Averaging male and female workers, someone employed 2,000 hours per year over a work life of forty years would earn $1.60 million. But with below-average looks the worker would earn only $1.46 million, while with above-average looks, lifetime earnings would be $1.69 million.[3] A 3 or 4 percent premium for good-looking workers doesn't seem that big; but placed into a lifelong framework, $230,000 extra earnings for being good-looking instead of bad-looking no longer seems small. Comparing the bad-looking to the average-looking worker the effect is smaller—"only" $140,000 over a lifetime—but still quite large. Comparing the average-looking to the above-average looking worker the effect is smaller still—"only" $90,000 over a lifetime—but still substantial.

All of these effects refer to averages: They tell us that a typical good-looking male will earn 4 percent more than the typical average-looking male, and that a typical below-average-looking woman will earn 4 percent less than the typical average-looking woman. This does not mean that *each* good-looking male will earn 4 percent more than each average-looking male. We have seen that there are many other factors that affect earnings, and these will differ between men whose looks are viewed as the same. Even more important, there is tremendous randomness in earnings that is unrelated to looks or any of the other things we can measure and that affect earnings. Among a randomly chosen group of male workers, or female workers, at least half of the differences in earnings are due to things that we can't measure; and among those that we can measure, looks account for only a small fraction of the differences. Looks do matter a lot; but other things matter much more.

Because so few people are classified as beautiful (rated 5) or homely (rated 1), it is not possible to distinguish statistically the impact of being beautiful from being above-average (rated 4), or of being homely from being plain (rated 2). Despite that, and even though the differences are not statistically meaningful, additional analyses of these same data show that the beautiful man or woman earns more than the above-average, and the homely earn less than the plain. Extreme looks are uncommon, but they generally produce extreme effects on success in labor markets.

The word "generally" is key here. Many people believe that a "bimbo effect" exists—that extremely good-looking women are somehow penalized in labor markets. In my own research I have found only one bit of evidence for this effect: In a study of attorneys, the very best-looking female attorneys were less likely to achieve partnership before their fifth year after graduation from law school than average-looking women attorneys.[4] Like their brethren, though, their extreme beauty did give them higher earnings. There may be bimbo effects in some instances, but they are pretty rare.

There have been many efforts to measure the effect of beauty on earnings using data on individuals in other countries. Interest in the topic is hardly limited to the United States. All of these have tried to adjust for many of the same determinants of earnings that I have used to isolate the effects of beauty in the United States. The availability of information on all these measures differs across countries and sets of data, so that the studies are neither entirely comparable to those from the United States nor to each other. They are also not comparable for another crucial reason: We saw that there are international differences in the willingness of raters of beauty to classify people as being below-average in looks. Americans are remarkably willing to make these relatively harsh judgments when they interview respondents or evaluate their photographs. This too might cause the estimated effects of beauty elsewhere to differ from those in the United States.

I have found studies for Australia; Canada; Shanghai, China; Korea; and the United Kingdom.[5] They show that in other countries too there are significant negative impacts on earnings of being below-average in looks. In most cases there are also positive effects of being above-average. No generalizations about cross-country differences in the effects of beauty on earnings are possible. But the negative effects of being below-average in looks typically exceed the positive effects of being above-average. One explanation is that so few people are classified as below-average in these studies that being called "below-average" indicates seriously deficient looks.

Although making comparisons of these effects to those shown in table 3.1 for the United States is difficult, the effects of beauty in other countries do not seem that different from those in the United States. The effects in the United States may be somewhat larger, but not hugely so. As in the United States, so too in most of these countries, good looks are rewarded, and bad looks are penalized, even after accounting for a large variety of other factors that affect earnings.

The American data clearly are somewhat outdated. With current data would we find the same effects? Perhaps Americans are no longer so concerned about looks when they react to co-workers, employees, or people selling them a product or a service. Perhaps the opposite has occurred, so that, given the preoccupation with looks in the American media today, with the rise of celebrity magazines, and with the growth of the social networking Internet site, Facebook, the effects are even greater than they were in the 1970s.

The absence of data makes it impossible to obtain updated estimates of the impact of beauty on earnings for the general population, but beauty ratings from a national survey of young adults in the early 2000s have been used to examine this question. Looking only at male high school graduates, going from "unattractive" (rating of 2 on the commonly used 5 to 1 scale) to "very attractive" (rating of 4) generated an increase in earnings of close to 11 percent among young women, and 17 percent among young men.[6] These effects are remarkably close to those in table 3.1, offering a hint that perhaps the effects of beauty on earnings remain substantial and substantially unchanged.

Without any additional evidence on the general population, there is no sure way of deciding this issue. Either possibility may be correct. My best guess, though, absent any reason to believe that labor markets have changed in one direction or the other, is that the effects of beauty today are not much different from those that prevailed in the United States in the 1970s.

The effects of looks on earnings might well change over the business cycle, as the economy moves between recession and full employment. From the employer's side of labor markets, having more unemployed workers available allows greater choice about workers' characteristics. In bad times, Cathy and Deb might have more scope to indulge their desires for beautiful workers. In discussing race in labor markets, we generally believe that unemployment gives employers more latitude to discriminate.[7] If looks are treated the same way, beauty might help a good-looking worker more during a recession, when there is more competition from other job seekers. Its effects will be less when workers are scarce and employers cannot afford to be so choosy.

No study has looked at this question generally. But among law school graduates who entered the labor market when jobs for new attorneys were very plentiful, the impact of differences in looks on their earnings was small. Among attorneys who sought work when jobs were less readily available, earnings were more strongly affected by differences in their beauty. This single comparison is not definitive, but it does suggest that the effects of beauty on earnings might rise in recessions.

IS BEAUTY THE REAL CAUSE?

There are a lot of other factors that might affect earnings and that could not be accounted for in most of these studies. One concern is that beauty may just reflect self-esteem. Perhaps people's self-confidence manifests itself in their behavior, so that their looks are rated more highly, and their self-esteem makes them more desirable and higher-paid employees. The Canadian study included a set of questions that psychologists use to measure self-esteem. Self-esteem and looks were positively related—but the correlations in these data were quite weak: The typical good-looking person was only slightly more likely to express substantial self-esteem than the typical bad-looking person. Adjusting earnings for the effects of self-esteem, workers who expressed greater self-esteem did earn more. But this additional adjustment did not change the estimated effects of looks on earnings in the Canadian data that had information on this characteristic. The constancy of the beauty effect suggests that its impacts on earnings do not arise because beauty enhances a worker's self-esteem.

Yet another possibility is that beauty and the attractiveness of one's personality are positively related, and that it is the general sparkle of one's personality, not one's beauty, that increases earnings. Measuring the attractiveness of someone's personality is more subjective than measuring someone's beauty, but both have been measured for the same group of young Americans early in the twenty-first century. Asking whether adjusting earnings for the attractiveness of personality affected the implied impacts of beauty, researchers found only a slight impact on young American adults.[8] The British study of beauty did adjust for measures of a person's sociability at age sixteen, and that adjustment didn't affect the estimates of the impact of beauty on earnings in adulthood either. Generally, the impact of beauty on earnings is essentially independent of any relation between beauty and personality.

It might be that the beautiful are more intelligent too, so that what we attribute to beauty is more appropriately attributable to intelligence. This is possible; but in light of popular discussion (the ugly nerd?), the opposite seems just as likely—that failing to account for differences in intelligence means that we might be under-estimating the impact of beauty on earnings.

None of the studies of random samples of Americans or people in other countries contains a good measure of intelligence, so we can't be sure about this. But the data on young adults in the United States in the early 2000s do contain a measure of intelligence. Adjusting for differences among individuals in both intelligence and beauty, those data show that the effect of beauty remains substantial even among people with similar intelligence. Interestingly, the premium for beauty is greater if you are smarter, as is the penalty for being unattractive.[9]

Looking at the same question in the context of a particular occupation, the data on attorneys included a partial measure of intelligence (the score on the Law School Aptitude Test—LSAT). There was no relation between a student's LSAT and his or her looks. This supports my guess that there generally is at most a tiny correlation between beauty and intelligence; so failing to account for intelligence doesn't affect the estimated impact of beauty on earnings.

In all the studies summarized so far, the assumption has been that the interviewers' ratings of beauty are based on the interviewees' faces. We made that assumption in chapter 2, arguing that observers can assess the beauty of a face independently of the weight and height of an individual. This is an important problem, for if they can't, and if weight and/or height affect earnings, then all the inferences made here so far would be confounding the effects of beauty on earnings with those of height and weight. So the first question is whether weight and height, or some combination of the two, even affect earnings.

Fortunately, a lot of research by economists and others over a long period of time, both in the United States and other countries, has looked at this. The answers seem fairly clear, for both weight and height. Obesity lowers earnings, all else equal, and that is especially true among women.[10] So if people judge the appearance of obese people as being below average—if obesity equals ugliness—the apparent negative effect of bad looks on earnings could just be masking the effect of being obese. Studies on the impact of height on earnings have also used data from many countries, including the United States, Britain, and China.[11] The general result is that height also matters, with the difference being that, unlike weight, the positive effects of height on earnings are larger among men than among women.

To disentangle the effects, we need to look at studies that include both beauty and weight/height to describe interpersonal differences in earnings. The American data underlying table 3.1, and the British study, included information on both height and weight. Adjusting for differences in the height and weight of the interviewees hardly changed the estimated effects of beauty on earnings. A study of job applications in Sweden similarly suggested that the impacts of beauty on the chance of a person getting a job interview were mostly independent of the effects of the applicant's weight.[12]

How can weight and height not change the impacts of beauty on earnings, if they themselves affect earnings? The answer is very clear and also encouraging: Observers are able to separate beauty from physique—the relationship between ratings of beauty and height/weight is very weak. Physiognomy and physique both affect earnings, but they are mostly independent of each other. A face on a tall or overweight body is judged about the same as the identical face on a short or thin body. Beauty is, within bounds, more or less independent of physique.

One might also wonder whether it is a person's beauty that is affecting his or her earnings, or whether beauty is just rated higher among those who are better dressed. Dressing better does raise perceived beauty, but only slightly; but perhaps those who dress better also earn more, so that some of the effect on earnings that we have attributed to differences in beauty stems instead from differences in dress. In several studies, earnings have also been adjusted for differences in dress (for examples, whether a man in a photograph was wearing a coat and tie, whether a woman was wearing a blouse). Having a photograph depicting oneself dressed more formally is associated with higher earnings. But, because the relationship between beauty and dress is quite weak, this additional adjustment hardly changes the inferences about the size of the impact of beauty on earnings. The beauty effect does not arise from any correlation of beauty and being better dressed.

WHY ARE BEAUTY EFFECTS SMALLER
AMONG WOMEN?

The careful reader will note that the estimated effects on earnings are larger for male workers than for female workers. This is true in the American data, and it is also generally true in studies for other countries. How can this be? Don't the beauty ratings summarized in chapter 2 suggest that people make finer distinctions about women's looks than about men's? After being presented with the results of some early studies in 1993, a leading observer of the role of beauty commented, "Women face greater discrimination when it comes to looks," essentially dismissing the facts that confronted her but that contradicted her preconceptions.[13] Albert Einstein's comment, "It is easier to split an atom than a preconception," is relevant in studying beauty too.[14]

For a variety of reasons, some of which I discuss in later chapters in various contexts, this dismissal, and these general beliefs, may be right, even though the inference that the earnings penalty for bad looks among women is larger than among men is also correct. To see why, ask what we would observe if both genders faced the same penalty on their earnings, say 10 percent for being below-average, and the same premium for having above-average looks, say 5 percent. Assume too that all adults were working for pay. What if there were also no differences by gender in the underlying distributions of beauty ratings (even though we know the ratings of women are more dispersed)? Then it would be the case that careful measurements of the effects of beauty on earnings would show that they are the same for women and men.

This point sounds reasonable, but it is wrong, because the assumption that all adults work is incorrect: Even in 2008, after a long rise in the fraction of adult women at work or looking for work (in the labor force), only 72 percent of American women ages 25–54 were in the labor force, compared to 86 percent of American men in that age group. Women are much more likely than men to stay out of the labor force. This is not surprising, since massive amounts of economic evidence demonstrate that women's decisions about whether to work for pay are more responsive to pay, other incentives, and the presence of young children than are men's.[15]

Gender differences in labor-force participation would be irrelevant here if non-participation were random—if the choice of staying out of the labor market were unrelated to beauty. But it is not reasonable to expect that the choice is random. People choose to work if the gains from working exceed the gains from staying at home. The gains from working are what you can earn—and beauty affects what you earn. The gains from staying at home are the enjoyment of leisure and the value to you and your family of what you do while at home (cooking, cleaning, fixing the plumbing, taking care of kids, watching television, etc.) and savings of costs for commuting and child care.

It is possible that better looks might make women so much more productive at home as to offset the pay gains they would obtain, but that seems unlikely. It seems much more likely that the incentives that beauty provides women to work for pay, and the disincentives that bad looks give women to avoid the labor market, are more important than differences in the value of time at home by looks. We would expect better-looking women to be working more than bad-looking women.

In the end, this is an empirical issue. One of the American data sets from the 1970s and the Canadian data allow us to infer the effects of beauty on whether women or men will choose to work or not. In both sets of data, there is no effect of either above- or below-average beauty on whether a man is working for pay. But being above-average in looks raises the likelihood that a woman works by about 5 percent compared to the average-looking woman. And the relatively small fraction of women whose looks are rated below-average are about 5 percent less likely than average-looking women to be in the labor market (and that much more likely to stay at home). The effects of looks on a woman's likelihood of working are not small, given that the average-looking woman ages 25–54 today has only a 72 percent chance of working.

A sign in a country store in Fredericksburg, Texas, read, "House work makes you ugly." That may be true; but the evidence also demonstrates that the reverse is true: Being ugly causes women to do house work, because the gains to working for pay are less than they are for better-looking women.

I made this point to a group of five hundred students, most of them Mormons, in a lecture at Brigham Young University. An unusually large percentage of female Mormon college graduates do not work for pay. The women attending the lecture were very upset with my comments, since they believed that, by noting that worse-looking women are less likely to work for pay, I was implying that Mormon stay-at-home moms are bad-looking. Not at all! If Mormon women's looks are no different from other American women's, the correct inference from the response of women to the disincentives to ugly workers to work, coupled with Mormon women's preference for staying at

home, is that Mormon stay-at-home moms will be better looking on average than non-Mormon stay-at-home moms.

This discussion and the evidence that supports it show
that one explanation for the surprisingly larger effect of looks
on men's than on women's earnings is that women have much
more latitude than men in choosing whether or not to work for
pay, and that beauty affects that choice. Part of the reason for
the gender difference in the effects of beauty on earnings is that
beauty alters the mix of female workers, so that the distribution
of workers contains proportionately fewer below-average looking women. That is less true for men.

DO BEAUTY EFFECTS DIFFER BY RACE?

The average beauty rating of African American respondents
is essentially identical to that of whites, but the dispersion of
the ratings is less. This might suggest that the effects of beauty
within the African American population might be smaller,
since mostly white employers and customers do not appear to
be able to distinguish beauty as well among black employees
as among whites. Perhaps; but unfortunately, there is no sufficiently large nationally random sample of data on which to
examine this possibility.

A bit of light is shed on the issue by evidence on the role
of African Americans' skin tone on their earnings. Skin tone
does not equate to beauty, but typical employers or customers
may treat it similarly to beauty. The evidence from a small random sample of African Americans suggests that light-skinned
African American males earn about 12 percent more than do
medium or dark-skinned black men, after adjusting for many

earnings-enhancing characteristics.[16] Perhaps beauty effects on earnings are just as large among African Americans as among whites.

DO BEAUTY EFFECTS DIFFER BY AGE?

Despite instructions to adjust for people's ages, observers are incapable of rating older people's looks as highly as those of younger people. Older people in the labor market are on average rated as less good-looking than their younger co-workers. Nonetheless, older people, generally up through age fifty-five or so, tend to earn more than younger people in the same occupation, industry, and location. The question, though, is: If we adjust for these differences and many others, does the impact on earnings of differences in appearance grow, stay the same, or decline as people age and gather more work experience? In succinct terms, how do the beauty premium and ugliness penalty in the labor market vary with age?

What might we expect the answer to this question to be? While average looks decline with age, the dispersion of looks— the variation around the declining average—doesn't change very much. It is just that there are more below-average people, and fewer above-average looking people. Thinking about this issue forces us to dig more deeply into the roots of the beauty premium in labor markets. Early in their jobs, workers are to some extent unknown quantities to their employers. The employer has interviewed them, examined their resumés, tested them, etc.; but their willingness to work hard, their attitudes, and how they get along with their fellow employees and customers are less well known to the employer. The employer, in screening them, may rely on their looks as an indicator of success along these other dimensions. Later on, once the employee has established a record of interacting with customers, other workers, and the boss, looks might become less important. The degree of uncertainty about the worker's true productivity should diminish over time. If that is true, then the impact of beauty on earnings will diminish with age and experience.

On the opposite side, early in a career good looks may give the worker access to more opportunities to build skills, meet customers, impress the boss favorably, and so on, than would be given to a worse-looking co-worker. The beautiful worker would have the chance to build her skills, perhaps with only small investments of her time. Skills are created through beauty in this case, but the enhanced skills are manna from heaven, in the sense that the worker has done nothing to create her additional earning power. Rather, the skills are thrust upon her by virtue of her good looks. In this case the effect of looks on earnings would rise with age, and it is a real effect, resulting from the growing skills that a worker's beauty generates over her career.

The evidence is mixed on this issue. Taking the data underlying the outcomes in table 3.1 and making the same adjustments for other factors, the premia for good looks, and the penalties for bad looks, are essentially the same for workers under and over age forty. This is not true in the data on attorneys. Following the attorneys over the first fifteen years of their careers, and adjusting for many of the factors discussed earlier in this chapter, there is a clear pattern. At the start of their careers, beauty has only a small effect on their earnings. The impacts of beauty on earnings rise with experience, which is very highly correlated with age in this group of attorneys.

One might think that beauty offers the young attorney advantages in building up a client base and that, as she acquires more experience, the work that she performed for clients who were attracted to her early in her career generates still more clients as her career progresses. This is the second possibility that I noted above. Among workers in occupations where earnings are less dependent on generating business, the effects discussed here may offset each other, as suggested by the absence of any difference in the earnings-beauty relationship by age in the United States generally. It is unlikely that there is any uniform pattern in the relationship between earnings and beauty across all countries and occupations. It depends on the specific nature of the occupation and on the specific factors that cause earnings to differ among its practitioners.

COMPENSATING THE BEAUTY-DAMAGED WORKER?

If you severely injured your back and couldn't work for years, your lost earnings would usually be compensated by the person or company whose negligence caused the accident. What if instead you were at work and a gas tank exploded, leaving your face severely scarred? Having read this far, you now know that your facial disfigurement means that you are likely to be earning less over the rest of your career. And if you had been severely disfigured in childhood, your entire career would have been different—your damaged looks would affect your earnings from the time you left school until retirement.

Should you be compensated for your potential loss of earnings? After all, your economic losses are just as real as if your back had been broken. My answer on this is yes; and the only economic question is how large your compensation should be. How much should you recover?

As soon as the first beauty study I wrote was made public and drew attention from the media, I began receiving calls from attorneys involved in personal-injury cases. In such cases, plaintiffs' attorneys seek damages for the impaired earnings suffered by their clients as a result of accidents. With the recognition of the labor-market payoff to beauty, the attorneys realized that the earnings lost because of the plaintiffs' impaired beauty were a previously unmeasured element of damages that they could obtain for their clients.

Over the years I have consulted in cases involving an executive injured in an oil-field explosion; several cases involving young children severely bitten by dogs; a child maimed in a hospital accident; and a number of others. Imagine a damaged face, perhaps that of a burn victim, or of a child permanently scarred by a severe dog bite. As an economist, my job is not to opine on the extent of the impairment to the victim's looks, but to assume a drop in beauty and provide an estimate of the size of the earnings losses that the individual had suffered based on that drop.

Typical approaches might involve assuming that an injured worker had been above-average in looks and that the injury reduced her looks to average; that she had been above-average and became below-average; or that she had been average-looking and became below-average looking. These three transitions capture the possible downward changes among the three categories of looks in table 3.1. I used the estimates in that table to infer the earnings loss that one victim, a woman who was thirty-six years old in 2009, suffered or will in the future suffer as a result of her injury.

To estimate the expected lifetime earnings that she would receive absent the injury, I assumed that she is typical for someone of the same race/ethnicity, education, and gender who resides in the same labor market. So if the victim had been a white male physician in a high-wage area—say, New York City—I would assume that his lifetime earnings would have been higher, absent the injury; if the victim had been a minority high school dropout working in a fast-food restaurant in South Dakota, they would have been lower.

We need to measure the earnings that she would receive in the possibly quite distant future, perhaps thirty years from now, and compare them to the compensation that she should receive in 2009. The solution is simple and standard in finance and economics: Discount the future dollars by some rate of interest to make them comparable to dollars today. For example, taking a standard interest rate of 3 percent after inflation, the earnings of $52,000 that she might receive in 2038, at age sixty-five, is equivalent in 2009 to only $20,000.

The magnitude of her loss depends on the severity of the impairment to her beauty. If she went from being above-average to below-average, the loss will be greater—because the difference in the impact on earnings of this change is larger than if she went from average to below-average. In her case, depending on how one views the severity of the impairment to her beauty, the present value of the lost earnings over her remaining working life is between $24,000 and $66,000.

In each case the size of the losses will vary. It is larger if the beauty impairment is greater, which is unsurprising. It is greater for men than for women, because the average unimpaired man earns more than the average unimpaired woman, and because the effects of differences in beauty on earnings are larger among men. The losses are lower for a seven-year-old than a fifteen-year-old, because the latter's lost earnings are in the nearer future. The thirty-six year-old woman's losses are not much bigger than a teenage girl's losses, because her injury occurred after she had already had the benefit of her looks over a substantial part of her career.

Is it worthwhile thinking about the economics of beauty in the context of injury-based lawsuits? Are these earnings losses really worth arguing about? By the criterion of net benefit to the plaintiff, the answer is a clear yes. The settlement or jury award might include one-half of the projected earnings loss from the impaired beauty. With my small fee, and the one-third of the settlement that is typically claimed by the plaintiff's attorney, even the smallest of the losses incurred by the thirty-six-year-old woman would net her about $7,000 beyond what would she have received had the economic effect of her impaired beauty been ignored.

LOOKS MATTER FOR WORKERS

The most heavily researched issue in the economics of beauty involves measuring the effects of looks on earnings. How much more do better-looking people earn than average-looking people? How much less do bad-looking people earn? The evidence on these questions is by now abundantly clear. Being in the top third of looks in America generates around 5 percent more earnings as compared to the earnings received by the average person who, except for beauty, is identical. People whose looks are in the bottom seventh earn perhaps 10 percent less than the otherwise identical average person.

In other countries, the impacts of looks on earnings may be smaller or larger than in the United States—it's hard to say. But that worse-looking workers earn less than their good-looking fellows appears to be a characteristic of industrialized countries generally. The same may also be true in less developed countries, and I think it is. But there just have not been enough studies of the impact of beauty in poor countries to confirm my suspicion. The effects differ across countries; but it is fair to say that the impact of looks on pay is universal.

CHAPTER 4

Beauty in Specific Occupations

BEAUTY AND CHOOSING AN OCCUPATION

You are almost certainly not going to choose to become an opera singer unless you have some natural vocal gifts; and you are not going to become a professional tennis player unless you have at least some basic level of physical coordination.[1] These are fairly esoteric occupations with few practitioners. Unlike vocal ability or physical coordination, beauty is a general characteristic. How does your beauty affect the occupation you choose to enter? It seems reasonable to believe that your beauty will help to determine the career choices that you make as a worker. To what extent are better-looking people choosing occupations where we think their looks might pay off more? Put crudely, does the old saying, "A beautiful face for radio," describe people's behavior generally?

If beautiful people tend to enter certain occupations, or if bad looks lead others to enter different occupations, how does this affect the payoffs to beauty in both types of occupation? More generally, are there differences across careers in the impacts that beauty has on their practitioners' incomes? For example, do good-looking lawyers attract higher fees? Do professors' looks matter for their salaries, or for how favorably their students evaluate their teaching?

The role of beauty is especially interesting in certain occupations. Prostitution, for example, is one area where we would think that beauty would matter a lot. Do good-looking politicians do better too—are people more likely to vote for beautiful politicians independent of their stands on the issues? In other occupations you might think that beauty would not matter at all. Why should it matter for professional athletes? Why should a good-looking criminal be more successful than an ugly one? Crime may not always pay; but does it pay to be a good-looking crook?

At first glance the "face for radio" *bon mot* suggests that beauty will not matter in radio broadcasting. Conversely, one might think that the effects of beauty will be large in occupations like door-to-door sales, movie acting, and electoral politics, where the "worker's" physiognomy confronts the buyer so directly. On one level these assumptions are correct: Most ugly people will not succeed as door-to-door salespeople, movie actors, or politicians, occupations where we think that there will be a premium on looks. Perhaps a bad-looking actor might make a living in a few character roles; but most ugly people, if they were required to become screen actors, would spend much of their time unemployed. The beautiful actors would earn much more than the hypothetical ugly actors, and we would see huge effects of beauty on earnings in screen acting.

Nobody is *required* to enter a particular occupation. We choose our occupations according to the advantages that we believe they will give us, both monetarily and in terms of the nonmonetary delights that they provide. Our choice of occupations is based on our preferences for different activities and our ability to perform different kinds of work. We sort ourselves among occupations based on this complex combination of preferences and productivities. And our success in various occupations is based in part on our characteristics, including our looks.

One of the leading television shows of the late 1980s and early 1990s was *L.A. Law*, a continuing drama centered on a group of attorneys and their practices and romances. Two of the main characters were played by Harry Hamlin, shown in figure 4.1, and Michael Tucker, shown in figure 4.2. I think that most people would regard Hamlin as better-looking than Tucker.[2] One of the two characters was a litigator, who spent a lot of time in court arguing in front of judges and juries. The other was a tax attorney, who spent little time in court. If you are not familiar with this show, guess which actor played which attorney?

Perhaps unsurprisingly, Hamlin was cast as the litigator, while Tucker was the tax attorney. By making these choices about casting, the series' executive producers implicitly recognized that people's good looks steer them into occupations where good looks will generate a bigger advantage, and that the absence of good looks leads them to enter occupations where looks are less important.

Looking at two pictures of actors portraying attorneys in a television series represents mere anecdote; and as a distinguished economist once told me, "The plural of anecdote is data."[3] In this case the precisely relevant data are available from the study of attorneys. In that survey the respondents were asked to list their legal specialty from among twenty-four choices, which were then summarized into four main categories.[4] Litigators (like the Hamlin character) were rated as the best

Figure 4.1. Harry Hamlin, American actor, 1990s. Photo by Alan Light.

Figure 4.2. Michael Tucker, American actor, 1990s. Photo by Alan Light.

looking based on photographs taken when they started law school. Attorneys in "Regulation and Administrative" specialties were rated the least good-looking, while those in "Corporate or Financial Law" or "Other" were rated somewhere in between. The Tucker character's specialty would have been classified as being in "Other" or "Regulation and Administrative."

This discussion makes it sound like only good-looking people will enter some occupations, while only plain people will enter others. Going still further, why doesn't the very best-looking 1 percent of workers enter the occupation that rewards beauty most generously? Why don't the ugliest 10 percent of workers wind up in those occupations where looks matter least? If people behaved this way, the effects of looks on earnings and on other outcomes within each occupation would be imperceptible, or at most tiny, since the distinctions among the looks of people in each occupation would be minute.

People do not choose to enter occupations based solely on their looks and on the potential payoffs to their looks in various occupations. Being good-looking would help an opera singer; yet not all opera singers are beautiful. Indeed, arguably the greatest soprano of the twentieth century, Maria Callas, was no beauty at all. Whatever her lack of good looks may have cost in success was far more than compensated by her extraordinary voice and musicality. As a more recent example, Dustin Hoffman's aunt told him, "You can't be an actor; you're too ugly." Yet two Best Actor Oscars have made it clear that looks are not the only thing that determines success in screen acting.[5]

We choose our occupations based on the mix of our skills, interests, and abilities, of which looks are just one. That choice is partly based on the importance attached to these different skills and endowments by the market, and beauty is only one of the

many things that are favored by the market. And it is favored
differently in different occupations. For this reason we will find
that the looks of workers within a particular occupation are not
all nearly the same. Characteristics other than looks also determine people's choices of occupation. We will, though, see less
variation in looks within an occupation than in the workforce
as a whole. On average, better-looking people will choose occupations where their looks pay off, and worse-looking people
will shy away from those occupations. The evidence for attorneys in different specialties demonstrates this fact.

Some anecdotal evidence for the notion that beauty can pay
off even with sorting across occupations is provided by a recent
example of an Italian priest who was organizing a web-based
beauty pageant for nuns, hardly a calling where we would think
that beauty is rewarded or even recognized by workers or "consumers."[6] Nuns could submit photos, and web-users would vote
for their favorites. The organizer said, "This contest will be a
way to show there isn't just the beauty we see on television, but
also a more discreet charm."

HOW BIG ARE BEAUTY EFFECTS WHERE
BEAUTY MIGHT MATTER?

A rapidly growing number of researchers have focused on how
differences in looks affect the outcomes that incumbents in various occupations experience. We have already discussed a study
of the effects of beauty on the earnings of attorneys, so let's look
at what the payoffs to beauty are in a variety of other occupations. In many cases the payoffs that have been measured are
purely monetary. In others, though, the research looks at how

workers' beauty affects their chance of success, as indicated by promotions or other measures of "getting ahead."

One occupation where beauty might matter a lot is prostitution. For the same service performed in the same kind of location, does a better-looking prostitute receive a higher price? This question has been studied by a number of economists who have interviewed street prostitutes, obtained information on their earnings and the kinds of activities performed, and had the prostitutes' looks rated by interviewers or panels of raters.

A regrettably unpublished older study is based on a detailed survey of street prostitutes in Los Angeles that interviewed more than 1,000 women.[7] The large majority of them were non-white or Hispanic, with few currently married, most never married, and only 20 percent with any college education. The women who were rated attractive earned about 12 percent more than the (majority of) women who were rated as less than attractive by the interviewers. This beauty premium is based on the price that the prostitute charged, after adjusting for all the women's other characteristics, as well as for the duration of their interactions with the clients and the kinds of sexual activity performed.

A study of prostitutes in several Mexican states compiled data on the price of the transaction and a rating of the woman's beauty (assessed at the end of the interview, and measured on the common 5 to 1 scale).[8] About 20 percent of the workers were rated as attractive (4 or 5) by their interviewer. These relatively attractive prostitutes obtained a price 19 percent higher than their fellow workers, even after the price was adjusted for the kinds of services performed, the other characteristics of the prostitute, and even her clients' characteristics. This seems like a huge effect, in light of all the other estimates presented in this and the preceding chapter. But maybe, even after women select into this occupation partly based on their looks, there is a large impact of beauty.

One of the authors of that study took the Mexican data and combined them with data on street prostitutes in Ecuador. The interviews and the assessments of beauty were obtained the same way as in the Mexican survey.[9] While the returns to beauty were not as large as those for the Mexican prostitutes, the Ecuadoran raters were much more generous in assessing beauty, leaving much less room for variations in looks to affect earnings. Taken together, the two studies demonstrate that, even within this occupation where you would think that beauty is crucial, selection into the occupation based on criteria other than looks allows differences in beauty to affect the amount that people earn.

Street prostitution is a risky business, as at least the initial contact between client and supplier must be made in public and with great uncertainty on both sides of the market. The risks involved are substantial, and it is possible that only those women who desperately want the income will be attracted to the occupation. If for whatever reason their attitudes toward risk are related to their looks, estimates of the impact of looks on prostitutes' earnings will be incorrect. A similar but much less risky occupation is that of escort. In that business the assignations are made more formally, more information is available to the purchaser, and there may be fewer risks to the escort. Earnings per hour are far higher than those obtained by street prostitutes, and the workers appear to be much better educated. With higher-income clients too, one might expect that workers in this occupation will be especially likely to be good-looking—richer clients will be able to purchase more beauty from the women providing the service.

The evidence suggests that this is exactly what happens. These sex workers are very young—over half under age twenty-six—and are disproportionately quite good-looking, at least as based on appraisals by their customers.[10] Yet even within this good-looking group, the better-looking among them earn more per hour for an identical set of services than do their less good-looking colleagues. With a move from the average to the 84th percentile of their looks comes an increase of 11 percent in the price charged (presumably also in the earnings that the escort retains from her services).[11] Here is an occupation where, perhaps more than anything except cinema or national television, customers are concerned about the workers' looks. Yet even in this job there is an extra payoff to especially good-looking workers.

Influence over events, honors, and monetary rewards are the benefits of success in an occupation—politician—where we would also think looks will matter. Today's candidates must appear on television and presumably need to look good to attract voters. One wonders, for examples, how George Washington would have fared speaking on television with his wooden false teeth; how Abraham Lincoln would have done with his saturnine looks; or how Theodore Roosevelt's high-pitched voice would have been received by television or radio audiences. In contemporary politics, one Republican political advisor noted, "If Sarah Palin looked like Golda Meir, would we even be talking about her today?"[12] Clearly, as the photographs of Nikki Haley and Barbara Mikulski shown in chapter 2 demonstrate, looks aren't everything in politics. But do looks even matter at all to a politician's success?

This question has been examined in a number of studies. For the United States, some researchers showed subjects brief flashes of videos of gubernatorial debates.[13] Based only on watching the videos, with the sound turned off, the subjects were able to predict the outcomes of the elections involving the two candidates fairly well. When sound was added, their ability to predict actually fell, suggesting that voters in the elections were at least in part focusing on differences in the candidates' looks.

A more direct approach was taken in a study of elections to office in the Northern Territory of Australia.[14] There the candidates' photographs accompany the paper ballots. Using beauty raters whose demographics mirrored those of the voting population, the authors showed that beauty had a statistically significant positive effect on the share of votes obtained by non-incumbents. The effect was also positive among incumbents, but not statistically significant. Once one accounts for candidates' party affiliations, however, the beauty effect essentially disappears. But skin color, which may be correlated with beauty ratings, and which we saw affects earnings of African Americans, then becomes an important predictor of electoral success. The bottom line here is that beauty matters, but that beauty ratings are complex combinations of a variety of characteristics, as we already knew.

While the effect of beauty did not seem large in these territorial elections, the same author also analyzed voting for seats in the Australian national parliament.[15] Here voters are presented with "How-to-Vote" cards by party workers, showing the name and almost always a picture of the party's entry in the constituency election. With a panel of evaluators of the pictures, the authors of the study were able to relate the average beauty rating of each candidate to his or her share of votes. Adjusting for the national strength of the candidate's party and for the candidate's incumbency and gender, the authors found that better-looking candidates, both incumbents and challengers, were more likely to be elected. Perhaps most interesting, it didn't matter how good-looking a candidate was, but only how much better- or worse-looking than the opponents the candidate was. Implicitly, voters compared the characteristics of candidates—both what they stood for (one hopes) and their looks.

A similar study was conducted on candidates for the German Bundestag (national parliament) in the election of 2002.[16] For candidates in each of a large number of parliamentary districts, the authors had a panel of observers rate the photographs that the candidates had supplied to the media. Given the source of the photographs, these were presumably the most flattering possible depictions, suggesting that there would be less variation in looks among the candidates' photos than existed in reality or that would exist among a random sample of Germans. Nonetheless, even after adjusting for party affiliation, the authors found that candidates whose looks were higher-rated obtained substantially and statistically significantly higher shares of the vote (and were thus more likely to win the election).

While the effect of beauty in the German election was substantial, in a study of a large number of Finnish elections the impacts of differences in beauty were extremely large for non-incumbent candidates. Going from the 50th the 84th percentile of looks (as rated by a very large panel of raters) would increase a candidate's number of votes relative to the average in a constituency by over 15 percent, even after adjustment for age, gender, and assessors' ratings of the candidates' competence and trustworthiness. In Taiwan the effects of differences in candidates' beauty were similarly large, especially among independent candidates, whose success did not depend on any help they may have received from political parties and may have been more tied to their looks.[17]

In all these studies it is clear that beauty matters for politicians. Politicos are right to do what they can to look better, to hire media consultants, to use the best possible photographs, etc. The media even give the better-looking candidate more publicity, and this pays off in elections.[18] Despite these efforts—despite what is probably selection into this occupation disproportionately from among better-looking citizens—we still find that there is enough variation in looks, and that beauty matters enough to voters, that being better-looking substantially enhances a candidate's chances of winning an election. The frequently observed smaller effects of looks on incumbents' electoral success suggest, though, that bad looks are less of an electoral impediment when voters have gained confidence in a politician.

An early study examined the earnings of a small group of recent MBAs over the first ten years of their careers, relating their earnings to their beauty as rated from pictures taken while they were in business school.[19] Better-looking men received higher starting salaries and experienced faster earnings growth over the decade. Among female MBAs, looks were unrelated to starting salaries, but better-looking women did see their earnings grow more rapidly (suggesting a rising effect of beauty with age).

Prostitutes, attorneys, politicians, and business executives all work in occupations where we would think that beauty will matter. People do select into these occupations based on looks, but the looks of people in the occupation are not all the same—

not all attorneys are good-looking. That variation in beauty within each occupation allows differences in beauty to pay off in higher earnings or a greater chance of getting ahead.

HOW BIG ARE BEAUTY EFFECTS WHERE BEAUTY MIGHT NOT MATTER?

My favorite occupations are university teacher and economist—the occupations I classify myself in. Does beauty affect outcomes in occupations like this, where we practitioners pride ourselves on valuing intellect over appearance? Take university teachers first. We saw in chapter 2 that students rating the looks of a group of professors in whose classes they had never been enrolled tended to rate them as being pretty bad-looking on average. The question is whether, within this less-than-pulchritudinous group, the better-looking people are more likely to get ahead.

We can measure the impact of beauty among professors in several ways. The first is the same way that we have measured its impacts in other occupations—by looking at its effects on earnings. A study of more than four hundred economics professors in Ontario, Canada, related their salaries to a measure of their "hotness": Whether or not students had assigned them chili peppers on the website www.ratemyprofessors.com.[20] Chili peppers are assigned when students think the professor is unusually good-looking, and in the Ontario study were "awarded" to about 10 percent of the professors. After adjusting for numerous other factors that might raise a professor's salary, including his or her age and publication productivity, the authors found that "hot" professors earned at least 6 percent more per academic year than their otherwise identical less good-looking peers.

Another way is to ask whether students like their courses—whether student evaluations are more positive for better-looking professors. The link between these evaluations and pay or promotion may not be direct or very strong. But university administrators do claim that they reward professors for good teaching, and, rightly or wrongly, most universities use teaching evaluations as the main measure of teaching quality. That better teaching performance generates higher pay is a mantra among university administrators—after all, they need to convince the customers that their opinions about the service-providers matter.[21]

In a study of professors at the University of Texas at Austin, whose looks were rated by students who had never met them, I found that the average student evaluation of the instructor's success in the course differed sharply by the professors' looks.[22] Going from the 84th to the 16th percentile of professors' looks in lower-division courses dropped the professor's rating from 4.4 to 3.6 on a 5 to 1 scale. Since two-thirds of the professors' ratings were between 3.5 and 4.5, this effect of differences in their looks was very large. The impacts were smaller in upper-level classes, perhaps because those students were more focused on substantive issues than students in introductory classes. This distinction seems similar to the difference in beauty effects between electoral incumbents and challengers.

One might be concerned that better-looking teachers are assigned to courses where students appreciate beauty more—where the student evaluations are more likely to be affected by the good looks of their instructor. Perhaps instructors in art history are better-looking than those in electrical engineering.

In this study, a large number of the classes were sections of the same course, so that for many courses the same kinds of students evaluated professors whose looks differed but who taught the same material. When we account for the particular course being taught, the impacts of looks on evaluations are actually a bit larger than those shown in table 3.1. There is no evidence that professors are assigned to courses or choose fields within academe based on their looks.

A similar approach was undertaken using instructional ratings of German university professors.[23] As in the American study, the ratings of beauty by a group of students (who were not in the professors' classes) were statistically significantly related to the evaluations that the German instructors received from the (different) students in their classes. While the impacts were not as large as in the United States, they were still substantial. No doubt the results would be different in other countries, for other kinds of students, and using different methods. But even in an occupation like college teaching, where we don't think beauty will be very important, differences in beauty produce impacts on an outcome that is arguably linked to economic rewards.

While we don't have studies of economists' beauty and their salaries, we do know something about the impact of their looks on non-monetary outcomes. In a profession that pays well, but that does not offer immensely higher monetary rewards to the top people, the distinctions offered by various honors become important. One such measure of distinction is the esteem in which they are held by their colleagues. In one study I examined how success in competitive elections to office in the American Economic Association, the leading professional organization in the field, is affected by the economists' looks.[24] Each voter (member of the association) receives pictures of the candidates along with the ballot, just as did the voters in Australia's Northern Territory, so that the candidates' looks confront you when you cast your vote.

Clearly, in such elections someone will win. So the relevant consideration is not the looks of the candidates alone, but instead, as with the Australian parliamentarians, how their looks compare to those of other candidates. The results show that moving from the 84th to the 16th percentile of looks lowers a candidate's chance of winning the election—of obtaining this honor—from 56 percent to 44 percent. This effect adjusts for measures of the candidates' scholarly productivity, their gender, and other characteristics. It suggests that even the choices of economists, many of whom like to think that they and their fellows are among the most rational people in the world, are affected by looks.

As a university professor and an economist, these studies do not make me happy. On a 5 to 1 scale I obtain teaching evaluations averaging 4.4 in my class of introductory economics, a score that is considered very good for a large course that is required for many freshmen. Yet if my looks were rated 9 on the 10 to 1 scale used in that study, the evidence suggests that my average teaching evaluation would be nearly 5. With that high a score I might be earning a higher salary! Similarly, if I were better-looking, I would have a much better chance of receiving one of the non-monetary rewards that my profession has to offer.

A recent study examined an occupation where we think that looks would not matter much at all—National Football League quarterbacks.[25] Having applied a computer program that measured facial symmetry in the quarterbacks' photographs, the authors related the symmetry measure to the athletes' annual salaries and bonuses, adjusted for their productivity (mainly passing yardage and years in the league). Going from the 84th to the 16th percentile of facial symmetry in this group of athletes reduced earnings by nearly 12 percent. That change is not far from the effect of decreasing beauty on men's earnings generally in the United States. This seems to be a pretty large effect for an occupation where you would think that only one thing—pure athletic prowess—would determine earnings.

In some occupations it might be possible that being bad-looking could actually give you an advantage, for example, in some criminal specialties. An ugly robber or thief might be more frightening to his potential victim than a good-looking one and might obtain the money and goods that he seeks more quickly and with less need for violence. Looks might be neutral in other criminal specialties. For example, since burglars do not expect their victims to see them, looks should not matter at all to a person's choice of becoming a burglar. In yet other criminal specialties, good looks should be quite important. A good-looking confidence man might have an advantage in conning his marks out of their savings. The diversity of illegal activities means that there is no reason to expect that crooks will be worse- or better-looking than the average citizen of the same age. Just as with attorneys, it depends both on the type of activity and, as is always true when people are making choices about occupations, on how beneficial good looks are in alternative occupations.

Based on a national survey that included beauty ratings, two economists examined how a young person's looks affected the chances that he or she engaged in criminal activities.[26] They considered the determinants of whether the young person had been involved in property damage, burglary, robbery, theft, assault, non-drug crimes, or selling drugs. Looks had very little impact on the chance that a youth had engaged in many of these criminal activities. But the small percentage of very unattractive youths were significantly and substantially more likely to have committed robbery, theft, or assault than were other youths. These are exactly the criminal activities where you would think that bad looks might lead to greater success. Their beauty was rated very early in their lives, so it appears that their ugliness led them into those criminal activities where it might have helped them; and it induced them to shun other, legal activities where it would have hurt their chances of success.

Even within occupations where you would think beauty doesn't matter, it does. Better-looking professors get higher teaching evaluations, better-looking economists get elected to offices in the professional society. Although it hasn't been studied, I would bet that better-looking radio announcers and disk jockeys (the "faces for radio") earn more than their bad-looking counterparts.

SORTING BY BEAUTY

Beauty affects who works at what, and how much they earn. But there is nothing unusual in this discussion about how personal characteristics affect people's choices of occupations and the returns to their skills and abilities. A similar discussion would apply if we were to analyze such characteristics as physical strength or musical ability. The same would be true about the impacts of workers' preferences, for examples, such as their attitudes toward risk or dislike of cold weather. What is special here is how pervasive the role of beauty is in labor markets. There aren't many occupations where tastes for weather really matter, for example, where those who dislike cold weather might earn more or less. Similarly, in most occupations one's musical ability has

no impact on earnings. Beauty, though, can have important effects in many occupations. And it does. It alters the choices that
people make about what occupation to pursue. Despite this,
within each occupation you find some people who are good-
looking and some who are bad-looking; and within most occupations, the better-looking earn more. Not immensely more,
but substantially and significantly more.

The essence of this chapter is conveyed in the following exchange from the November 16, 2004, episode of the television
series *House*:

House: Would that upset you, really, to think that
             you were hired because of some genetic gift of
             beauty, not some genetic gift of intelligence?
Cameron: I worked very hard to get where I am.
House: But you didn't have to. People choose the
             paths that grant them the greatest rewards
             for the least amount of effort. That's the law
             of nature, and you defied it. That's why I hired
             you. You could have married rich, could have
             been a model, you could have just shown up
             and people would have given you stuff. Lots
             of stuff, but you didn't, you worked your
             stunning little ass off.

Dr. Cameron chose to go to medical school because she wanted
to—being a doctor mattered most to her. The evidence here
suggests that her choice of emergency medicine—with lots of
patient contact—is a good one for her to take advantage of her
beauty. Dr. Cameron's good looks will benefit her in her medical career too.

CHAPTER 5

Beauty and the Employer

THE PUZZLES

In many occupations better-looking workers earn more than others, while bad-looking workers do worse than average. Across the entire economy, good-looking workers earn more on average than their otherwise identical but less well-endowed colleagues. A crucial puzzle is how employers of these workers can survive in a competitive market, if their workers, who are no different from others except for their looks, are paid more. How can they compete against other employers in the same industry who are willing to settle for the less expensive, uglier workers?

Take, for instance, Alan Greenspan, former Chairman of the U.S. Federal Reserve Board. Before his full-time public service, he headed an economics consulting company for which he hired mostly female economists. He did not institute this hiring policy out of any particular desire to surround himself with women, nor out of charity aimed at women generally. Instead, when asked about it, he pointed out that the women were just as good workers as men and, because they were cheaper to hire due to discrimination in the labor market, he could make more money for the company by employing them. He was willing to take advantage of the discriminatory behavior of other employers toward female economists in order to make his own company more profitable. But how could those other consulting companies survive when bidding for contracts against Greenspan's company, which could offer equally high-quality services at a lower price because its labor costs were lower? Moving from anecdote to data, some recent evidence shows that start-up companies that employed more women survived longer than others.[1] More generally, how can companies that fail to employ otherwise identical but lower-paid female, minority, or ugly workers survive?

A different puzzle is how the beauty of the entrepreneurs themselves affects their companies' success. How do employers' looks affect the performance of the companies they head? Thinking about and obtaining evidence on this point might allow us to understand better the sources of the economic impacts of beauty.

I documented the effects of differences in beauty on pay with a large number of research studies conducted by many authors. Evidence on the puzzles here is much sparser. That means that the conclusions are necessarily more speculative and rest on the strength of the arguments as much or more than on a large body of carefully obtained evidence.

DO GOOD-LOOKING EMPLOYEES RAISE SALES?

I discussed this question with a class of freshmen and asked whether they cared about the looks of employees at the companies they dealt with. One young woman said that she certainly does care, and that, for example, she would not buy cosmetics from a salesperson who was not well groomed and at least decent-looking. The brand of cosmetics that she chooses to buy may be the same no matter who sells it. But presumably the saleswoman's looks will convey something to my student and others about the product that would make buying it more or less desirable to her.

Cosmetics manufacturers recognize the link between their products' sales and beauty and make special efforts to obtain unusually attractive spokeswomen. Indeed, some of the greatest beauties of the past fifty years have been seen on television, movie advertisements, and billboards as representatives of cosmetics lines. The succession of beautiful women includes such stars as Catherine Deneuve, Isabella Rossellini, Kate Winslet, and Anne Hathaway—all presumably recruited because the companies believe that customers will find them attractive, identify with them and purchase the products they endorse.

A good-looking attorney might be able to attract more clients and bill more hours, at higher hourly fees, if potential clients believe that he is more likely to be successful on their behalf. The attorney may be no better at writing briefs, doing legal research, or developing oral arguments, but clients may believe that he will be more likely to prevail before a judge or jury, or in negotiations with other attorneys. In a very real sense the legal service is tied to the attorney's looks, just as the cosmetics product was tied to the endorsers'.

If we think of looks as part of a product or service, and if we assume that potential customers value looks, then it is clear how better-looking employees can raise a competitive company's sales. At the same average cost of all the other inputs into the product and at the same price charged, customers will be more likely to buy the product and/or will be willing to buy more of it. More will be sold; and the company will expand at the expense of its competitors. If the company has some control over the prices it charges, the argument is even stronger: Tying its product or service to a better-looking provider will enable it to sell at a higher price and/or sell more, even though the product is little different from the one offered by another company. But regardless of the kind of market where it operates, a company that can tie its goods and services to better-looking workers will be able to increase its price, the amount it sells, or both, and thus increase the total value of its sales. The beauty of the seller becomes an integral part of what the company offers.

All of these examples imply that beauty is somehow productive to the company—that it raises sales because customers are willing to pay more to buy products and services provided by beautiful workers. An alternative is that beauty is unproductive to the company—that it doesn't affect the company's sales, and that it is instead a characteristic that bosses are willing to pay for in order to have the pleasure of interacting with good-looking employees. As Jade Jagger, jewelry designer and daughter of Mick, exclaimed, "God, what gorgeous staff I have. I just can't understand people who have ugly people working for them."[2]

To examine whether in fact beauty raises sales, one study looked at the effect of Dutch advertising executives' beauty on their companies' revenues.[3] At the time covered by the data (the mid-1980s through mid-1990s), the Dutch advertising industry included many companies, with most of them, including nearly all the larger ones, located in the area covering the major cities of Amsterdam, Rotterdam, Utrecht, and The Hague. While the industry was competitive, in the sense that there were many firms, with no single firm having a share of the market even approaching 10 percent, many of the companies had niches where they had some ability to determine price.

The companies' executives (directors in local parlance) run their company, engage in creative activities, and market their products. Their beauty, based on their photographs, was rated by a panel of four adults on the 5 to 1 scale. Combining all companies together, moving from the 84th to the 16th percentile of average looks of executives across the companies was associated with a decrease in sales of 7 percent. Clearly, having better-looking executives in a company in this industry generates fairly substantial increases in sales.

This study inspired a cartoon in a Dutch newspaper, showing a grossly deformed woman looking at a pretty executive and thinking, "If that's how things go, then even I can do it!"[4] But the evidence would suggest that she cannot, if "it" is bringing in more business and inducing subordinates to work harder. She may have the same education and the same tangible skills as the good-looking incumbent seated at the desk, but her obviously deficient looks would make her less productive to the company—she would not generate as much revenue.

One difficulty with this study is that the people whose beauty is linked to the companies' sales are not just the companies' employees—they are also its managers. They may function as entrepreneurs in these firms as well as drawing salaries as employees. So part of the effect of their beauty is not only to increase their company's revenue directly, but perhaps also to change its direction in a way that raises sales.

No studies are available of workers who function only as employees of profit-making companies and whose work as an employee might raise their company's sales. But one study did examine the ability of employees in a non-profit organization to generate revenue.[5] The research examined the success of door-to-door solicitors, typically lower-skilled part-time workers, in raising funds for a particular charity. One of its aims was to estimate the effects of the solicitors' looks on the amounts of funds raised, and for that purpose the researchers had pictures of each solicitor rated by many individuals on a 10 to 1 scale.

The differences in success rates arising from differences in the looks of the male solicitors were tiny. But among female solicitors beauty mattered a lot, with an increase from the 16th to the 84th percentile of female solicitors' looks nearly doubling the likelihood of receiving a contribution, and increasing the expected contribution by nearly two-thirds. Better-looking female solicitors got more people to contribute, although the additional contributors were those who had been on the fence between giving nothing and giving only a small amount.

In an extension of this study, one of the authors used the same data to see whether certain aspects related to looks have distinctive effects on the solicitor's success.[6] Holding constant the rating of the solicitor's looks, he asked whether a female solicitor's hair color affected her success. It clearly did: Blonde solicitors were substantially more likely than other female solicitors to elicit a contribution, and the average amount raised per contact was higher too. Their greater success occurred because of their greater appeal to Caucasian contacts. These results underscore the central role of interactions between the worker and the customer that were illustrated in the discussions of attorneys, politicians, and prostitutes.

The inference from these studies is that having better-looking employees does increase a company's sales. Advertising firms' customers apparently prefer to deal with better-looking

ad executives, allowing the latter to charge more for their services. Ordinary home-dwellers prefer to contribute to a chari-
table cause when approached by a better-looking fund-raiser.
Generalizing from two studies to an entire economy is prob-
lematic; but the evidence does suggest that the extra costs that
a company incurs when it pays for better-looking workers are
at least partly offset by the greater sales that those workers can
generate for it.

HOW DOES BEAUTY AFFECT PROFITS?

With its workers' beauty raising a company's revenue and costs,
the question the company faces is whether the increased revenue justifies the increased costs. A company should keep adding
workers, presumably in descending order of beauty, until the
last worker hired generates just enough extra sales to offset the
extra pay that his good looks require. The average (based on
looks) employee in the firm might add more to sales than to
wage costs—we might find that the average worker's looks do
raise the employer's profits. But the beauty of the ugliest worker
hired should be a wash—the company should be indifferent between hiring him and a worse-looking worker.

This discussion assumes that companies understand the role
of beauty in affecting their revenue and their costs. Of course,
nobody would argue that every employer or even many employers make explicit calculations comparing the gains resulting from a particular worker's beauty to the extra labor costs
his beauty may engender. They do not need to. As long as some
companies implicitly account for how beauty affects costs and

revenue, they will make extra profits. Employers in their industry who fail to make the correct decisions about the effects of beauty on their sales and costs will make less profit. They will lose out to their competitors, and, in the end, only those companies that account for the role of beauty will survive.

Does this economic approach really describe the implied benefit-cost calculations that employers make? There is no way of knowing whether it does for employers in general or, indeed, for most employers in specific. As always, all we can do is provide examples for a few companies; and in this case the evidence is again sparse.

Employers do explicitly seem to believe that they will be helped if they hire better-looking workers. In countries where, unlike in the United States, help-wanted advertisements can specify personal characteristics, including beauty, we see employers specifically mentioning beauty in seeking applicants. In China, for example, a recent study of these advertisements showed a requirement for looks being mentioned nearly 10 percent of the time, with a much greater prevalence in lower-skilled jobs.[7] Some ads in Mexico even require that job applicants submit photographs to demonstrate that they have a "nice appearance."[8]

To examine the impact of beauty on profits, take the Dutch advertising data. Moving from the 16th to the 84th percentile of executives' looks raised sales by about $60,000 in 2009 U.S. dollars. Assume, following the evidence on the effects of beauty on earnings, that this large a difference in beauty raises executive pay by 15 percent. In 1994, a Dutch worker earning the equivalent of $175,000 would have been among the top 1 percent of earners. That earnings level is an upper limit to the earnings of the average-paid executive in the sample, since there are proportionately many fewer very high earners in the Netherlands than in the United States.[9] The maximum impact of beauty in the average firm could have been no larger than $25,000—less than half of the average impact of beauty on firms' sales. In this, the only study of the issue, the effect of looks on companies' sales far exceeds its impacts on their costs.

Since profit is the excess of revenue over cost, this evidence implies that good-looking workers raised the firms' bottom lines. Fine, but how can this be true? If I were a good-looking worker, and I realized that the company was making profits off my good looks, I would feel that I was being exploited and would insist on being paid what I was worth. If my demands were not met, I would take my good looks elsewhere to get paid the amount that I am adding to my company's revenue. I might not do this immediately, but eventually I would. Even if I did not leave the company, potential new good-looking workers would realize the value of their looks and insist on being paid what they are worth. Why doesn't this appear to happen? Why don't workers compete away the profits that their beauty seems to generate?

One possibility is that most workers simply are not aware of the contribution of their looks to their company's revenue, and they allow themselves to be exploited. This explanation not only assumes some ignorance on the part of workers, but also that their employers are smart enough to take advantage of them. Perhaps so, but this is not a very satisfying explanation—claims of irrationality or poor information are not very appealing and imply that companies and/or workers are too dumb to be aware of their own interests.

One explanation that is consistent with companies and workers possessing good information about the impact of the workers' beauty is that beauty, especially of a senior worker, grows into an asset that is shared by the worker and the company. A good-looking worker joins a company and helps to build up a team of other workers. Like all of us, the other workers are charmed by their fellow employee's good looks and are themselves spurred to greater productivity. Were the good-looking worker to leave, her team would disintegrate and lose its *esprit*, so that the remaining workers would become less productive than before. But if the good-looking worker went elsewhere, she would have to start anew in building up a group of workers whose productivity would be enhanced by her looks. According to this explanation, the worker's looks essentially represent hers and the company's beauty capital. It is something whose benefits, even though they are embodied in the good-looking worker, are partly specific to the company where she has been working.

The returns to this beauty capital are shared by the company and the worker.[10] She cannot ask for the entire returns to this kind of capital, because, if she leaves the company, the value of the beauty capital that she takes with her is diminished. The company could grab all the returns and pay her nothing for the extra value created. But in doing so, the employer would increase the chance that she would simply quit, killing the beautiful goose that has laid golden eggs. A solution is to share the returns to this asset, which is the result of the worker's inherent good looks and the company's having assembled a team of co-workers whose productivity is enhanced by those good looks.

This explanation only works to the extent that the good-looking worker is in a position to inspire her co-workers. If she works alone, she could not create this kind of shared capital. This approach suggests that opportunities for the mutually advantageous use of good-looking workers are greater in jobs where the good-looking worker has more co-workers and also has more contact with them. This may be one more reason why good looks pay off: Supervisory jobs, where the worker must explicitly deal with other workers, pay better. The inspirational role of beauty in the workplace is a reason why better-looking workers are more likely to be promoted into supervisory positions.

Can companies take advantage of differences in their executives' looks to increase sales and raise profits still further? Ask yourself: Would a company that had two executives rated 3 on the 5 to 1 scale have higher or lower sales than a company with one executive rated 5, the other rated 1 on that scale?

When I was working on the study of Dutch advertising companies' sales, my Dutch coauthor and I started wondering about this question. I bet him five guilders (less than $3—hardly a Vegas-size bet) that greater dispersion of looks among a company's executives would be associated with additional sales. My reasoning was that, with one homely and one beautiful executive, the company could increase sales by having the good-looker out bringing in clients and the homely exec in the back office designing layouts for advertisements. With two average-looking executives the company cannot profit from the comparative advantages possessed by the executives along the dimensions of their appearance and other skills. I won the bet: Companies whose executives' looks differed more from each other had higher sales. It's not only having good-lookers that raises sales and profits; it's having a beneficial mix of executives ranked by looks and making sure that they specialize in tasks that take advantage of differences in their looks.

HOW CAN COMPANIES PAY FOR BEAUTY AND SURVIVE?

The answer to the titular question in this section is easy: They survive because their workers' good looks enhance their profits. The extra wages paid to the good-looking workers are more than offset by the extra revenue that the workers' looks help to generate. This conclusion is, as noted earlier, based on one study, the only one available; but it does answer the question about survival. The problem is that it answers it too well: If good-looking workers raise profits, why aren't firms that employ a disproportionate number of good-looking workers driving out the other firms in their product markets that choose, for whatever reason, to rely on uglier workers?

One answer to this question is to conclude that one study does not a proof make. We really don't know very much about whether a worker's beauty generates enough extra sales to more than cover the extra wage costs that it imposes on the employer. In the end we do not yet know whether companies that employ better-looking workers are expanding at their competitors' expense, are breaking even, or are losing out to competitors who have chosen the ugly-worker route in hiring. There just is not enough research to answer the question. What we do know, though, is that it is perfectly reasonable to think that companies that employ better-looking workers may not only survive—they may flourish at the expense of their competitors.

DO COMPANIES WITH BETTER-LOOKING
CEOS PERFORM BETTER?

In 1996, the editors of a weekly Swiss business newspaper, *Cash*, having seen some of the earlier research on beauty, decided to hold a contest among their readers. Each reader could cast a vote for the best-looking CEO in Switzerland.[11] This resulted in nine hundred votes, with the amazing result that the CEO of the company that published the newspaper was rated best-looking! The newspaper apologized profusely for the seeming phoniness of the contest results, and it did point out that the second-, third-, and fourth-most favored CEOs headed three of the biggest companies in the country, including the international pharmaceutical giant Novartis and the food conglomerate Nestlé. The other top winner changed jobs shortly after the contest and rapidly rose to become CEO of Deutsche Bank, one of the world's largest banking corporations.

Except for the top vote-getter, the winners headed companies that tended to be larger than those headed by the CEOs of most of the companies included in the contest. This was hardly a scientific study, but it does suggest a positive correlation between a company's success and its CEO's looks. This may just be the result of sorting: Boards of directors of already successful corporations may prefer to have a pretty face representing the corporation and may be willing to pay for it. But it could just as likely show a causal relationship—the good-looking CEO may raise the revenue of the firm he or she heads.

A pair of psychologists showed pictures of the CEOs of the top 25 firms in the Fortune 500, and of CEOs of the firms ranked 476 through 500, to a large group of undergraduate students.[12] The students rated the executives' facial features along a number of criteria, including their overall attractiveness. Appraisals of the power implied by the faces were more positive for executives in the larger companies. Although the faces of the CEOs of the largest and smallest companies did not differ statistically in their attractiveness, the larger companies' CEOs were rated as somewhat better-looking.

This evidence provides only very weak support for the anecdotal evidence from the Swiss survey. Why isn't the support stronger? First, while there are substantial agreements on what constitutes human beauty, those agreements are by no means perfect; and a set of undergraduates is hardly the group whose views on beauty are likely to match well those of the typical Fortune 500 company's customers, whose tastes presumably affect corporate boards' appointments of CEOs. A second problem is the same as that noted for the Swiss beauty contest: This kind of study says nothing about causation. Even if there were a strong positive relationship between looks and company size, the most that we could say is that the relationship might be causative, or it might simply result from the better-looking executives being sorted into the larger companies.

As much as one would like to claim that beauty leads to CEOs generating extra profits for their companies, the only evidence on this point is suggestive. The real problem here is the common one in the now immense literature on the productivity of CEOs. It is difficult enough to demonstrate a strong correlation between a company's profits and its CEO's compensation. Demonstrating a causal relationship from CEO pay to a company's sales and/or profits is much, much harder.[13] That being the case, how much more difficult is it then to show that a particular characteristic that CEOs may possess—their looks—is causally linked to their firm's performance? Even with substantially more than the current sparse research, we are not likely to be able to understand the effects of a boss's beauty on a company's success with as much precision as the impact of workers' beauty on their earnings.

BEAUTY HELPS COMPANIES—PROBABLY

The best guess based on research on the relation of employees' and bosses' looks to their company's success is that having better-looking workers helps the company chalk up greater sales. It even seems possible that the improvement in sales is so great as to overcome, and possibly even exceed, the extra costs created by the extra pay that a company must offer its better-looking employees. Because of this at least offsetting effect on revenues, companies can survive and perhaps even make extra profits by employing more costly, better-looking workers. From the typical company's narrow point of view its employees' beauty can be productive—it can raise profits.

What is the bottom-line implication for companies—should they actively seek out better-looking workers in the belief that their extra cost is more than offset by the extra revenue that their looks will help generate? More than in most discussions, the academic caveat—more research is needed—applies here. Nonetheless, the sparse evidence does tell employers that they should look for better-looking workers, since the good-lookers appear to generate more extra revenue than their extra pay costs their employers. If enough employers followed this suggestion, though, the workings of the market would soon make this advice worthless. Companies would move to the point where the marginally good-looking workers would be paid just enough more than worse-looking workers to offset any additions to sales produced by their looks. The implication is clear: Be the first one in your industry to hire the good-lookers. But watch out: Eventually your competitors may do so too and compete away the advantages you had gained for yourself.

CHAPTER 6

Lookism or Productive Beauty, and Why?

WHAT THE BEAUTY EFFECT MEANS

Beauty raises earnings, in the population in general and among practitioners in particular occupations. There is no question that it benefits the beautiful; and we saw how it increases companies' sales, and perhaps even their profits. Beauty provides extra money for those who possess it and is productive for those who hire them; but is it productive for society? How can we discuss the effects of beauty in terms that economists, attorneys, and the general public might find useful? Do they result from discrimination, and if so, who is discriminating? What does it mean for beauty to be productive? Underlying these questions is the central one: *Why does beauty matter for individuals, companies, and even the economy as a whole*?

One possibility is *lookism*—pure discrimination in favor of the good-looking and against the bad-looking—that should concern every citizen. By this view, companies benefit by hiring the beautiful because they can cater to people's discriminatory preferences, but their behavior harms society. The other possibility is that it not only benefits companies to hire the beautiful; it is *socially productive*. By this view, beauty is no different from any other inherent characteristic, such as intelligence, physical strength, or musical or artistic ability, that makes workers more appealing to potential employers and that makes their product inherently better. But before attempting to distinguish the ultimate causes of the beauty effects, we need to understand what is meant by the economic categories—discrimination and socially productive. Both have various meanings in different contexts, but we need to give them precise meanings in order to allow us to differentiate among the possible sources of the effects of beauty on workers and companies.

HOW CAN BEAUTY EFFECTS BE DISCRIMINATION?

One dictionary defines discrimination as, "a. The act, practice, or an instance of discriminating categorically rather than individually. b. A prejudiced or prejudicial outlook, action, or treatment."[1] One crucial term here is "categorically," which in this case suggests that people are being classified by their looks rather than by their other, individual characteristics. The other is "treatment"—disparate behavior toward workers that leads to a disparate impact on them, in this case, to outcomes in labor markets that are different and that depend on workers' looks. The central paradigm in the discussion of labor-market discrimination in economics starts with outlook—preferences, essentially the second definition. It then moves, to impact, essentially the first definition. The idea goes back to 1957 to the doctoral dissertation of Gary Becker, Nobel laureate in economics in 1992.[2]

Following Becker's basic theory, economists view discrimination as a preference against buying from, employing, or generally dealing with people in a particular group. Preferences against members of Group U (Ugly) differ across employers (assume for now that we are talking about employers' choices). Some employers might not care about their employees' looks—might not discriminate. After all, the U workers produce as much as B workers; but how are all of the Ugly workers going to find jobs if there are only a few non-discriminatory employers? The only way is if they can make hiring themselves advantageous to other employers. And the only way to do that is by accepting lower wages, by bribing employers to overcome their prejudices against the ugly.

How much will it take to conquer other employers' prejudices? With just a few more U workers than non-discriminatory employers, the wage difference between U and B workers will be small. Even the last U worker to get a job will be working for an only slightly bigoted employer. But as the size of Group U expands relative to the number of non-prejudiced employers, U workers will need to accept jobs from an increasingly prejudiced group of employers if they want to work.

In the end, the pay of U workers will be determined by the prejudice of the employer who is the most prejudiced among those employers who are willing to hire U workers. Prejudice among the most bigoted employers of all will not affect the pay of U workers—the U workers won't bother approaching those employers. Instead, it is the preferences of employers who are willing, at some reasonable price, to accept a bribe in the form of lower labor costs to overcome their distaste for hiring U workers which determine the U workers' pay shortfall.

The penalty (the wage discrimination) suffered by U workers is determined by employers' preferences about the type of workers they wish to employ and by the relative size of Group U. How does this relate to the wage penalty suffered by bad-looking workers and the wage premium received by good-looking workers? Assume first that all workers are identical along every dimension except that of looks. Also assume that employers can divide workers into the three groups—good-looking, average, and bad-looking—that most studies have looked at.

The outcomes in the labor market are clear: Whatever the good-looking workers earn, the average-looking workers must accept lower earnings in order to compensate employers for their inferior looks; and the bad-looking workers must accept still less. Whether good-looking workers receive premium pay, or their pay is the basis against which to calculate pay penalties in the other groups, is irrelevant. We can't tell if good-looking workers are being favored, or if bad-looking workers are being penalized. Regardless, we can view the pay differences as reflecting discrimination.

Talking about this kind of discrimination as if its source were the prejudices of employers who choose which workers to hire is just an expositional convenience. It could equally well stem instead from the prejudices of workers generally: The average worker might refuse to work next to a bad-looking co-worker and only be willing to work if compensated, in the form of a higher wage, for looking at an ugly colleague for eight hours per day. The outcome would be the same as if employers' prejudices were responsible. Bad-looking workers would earn less than average-looking workers; and good-looking workers would command premium pay, as they make the workplace more appealing to other workers and so enable employers to hire other workers for less pay.

The phenomenon could equally well stem from consumers' prejudices. Even if people do not discriminate in their roles as workers or employers, if they discriminate as consumers—if they prefer to deal with better-looking professors, salespeople, television-presenters, athletes, or entertainers—better-looking people who are otherwise identical will earn more in any activity in which they contact consumers. Bad-looking workers will shy away from those occupations and move into other occupations where looks do not matter as much. That will reduce earnings for everyone in those other occupations, but the effect will be biggest for the bad-looking workers, since they would constitute a disproportionate share of workers in those other occupations.

This discussion has been based on the most widely accepted theory of discrimination—that discriminatory outcomes arise from preferences against individuals who differ from others along the dimensions of certain characteristics, such as race, gender, ethnicity, religion, sexual preference, or, in this case, looks. Economists have developed other theories of discrimination. Whether these additional ideas are useful in discussing the inferior outcomes experienced by bad-looking workers is worth considering, since they might shed additional light on the role of looks in labor markets.

One variant of the basic theory of discrimination ignores preferences and instead assumes that we categorize other people into groups about which we have stereotypes that lead us to expect different behavior. This idea, known as statistical discrimination, and owing originally to the work of Edmund Phelps, economics Nobel laureate in 2006, and others, suggests that members of the group that is discriminated against are assumed to be less productive on average than other workers.[3] While a few group members can overcome the stereotype by demonstrating their high productivity, most cannot, and they are all lumped together as being less productive than members of other groups. A few group members might do well, but most will earn less than other workers because employers and perhaps others too assume that their membership in the group signals that they are less productive than other workers.

Statistical discrimination is very appealing as a description of how we view groups of people generally; but it is not a satisfactory way of describing the lower earnings of bad-looking workers. Employers or others may lump good-looking workers into one group and bad-looking workers into another, and assume that the latter are on average less productive than the former. But this view seems far-fetched as compared to a simple preference-based approach. Instead, it seems more reasonable to assume that, without some compensation in the form of lower wage costs, employers would not want bad-looking workers around; and customers would not buy from them at the same price of the product or service. This view fits the preference-based theory of discrimination more closely than a theory of statistical discrimination.

A second variant on the basic theory of discrimination is that there is crowding into some occupations. The notion is that employers get together to force members of the discriminated group into certain occupations (or alternatively, keep them out of other occupations). This keeps wages in these occupations artificially low due to the crowding of workers into them.[4] The occupations might be such now-antiquated ones as clerk-typist, in the case of women, or railroad sleeping-car porter, in the case of African Americans. This approach requires some kind of collusion among employers to force group members into particular occupations. As with statistical discrimination, it may be useful generally; and we know that beauty matters more in some occupations than others. But, since it seems unlikely that employers get together and plot to force ugly workers into certain occupations, it is not as desirable a way of describing discrimination based on looks as the simpler preferences-based approach.

HOW CAN BEAUTY BE SOCIALLY PRODUCTIVE?

The sparse evidence suggests that beauty is privately productive—it raises sales in the companies that hire good-looking workers. Preferences for beauty benefit the beautiful and help their employers sell more. That is productivity in a narrow, private sense—it says nothing about whether society is better off because of people's preferences for beauty in their economic transactions. But that is the issue—is the benefit of beauty to good-looking people and their employers of any value to society as a whole?

First consider intelligence. There are numerous kinds of intelligence, be it skills at mathematics, ability to solve puzzles, social skills, or others.[5] Possessing any of these might raise an individual's productivity, no doubt more so in some jobs than in others. Your mathematical skills might enable you to calculate trajectories of rockets more rapidly, argue more logically in a legal case, or even prove theorems in mathematical economics. Your ability to solve puzzles might make you a better engineer. Your social skills might enable you to induce other people to agree to your requests, or to manage the skills of other people more successfully and thus raise a company's sales.

Each of these forms of intelligence is to a large extent inherent in the individual who possesses it. Each raises a person's productivity in the workplace—the amount that the person adds to his or her company's sales. This added productivity is marketable and induces employers to bid for the person's services, so that those who possess the skill will receive higher pay than those who do not. We believe that the intelligent are paid more because they produce more for their employers. But we also believe that this extra production benefits society, in the form of technological advances, more efficient organizations, and even better economic research.

Good-looking people also earn more and also create more sales for their employers. Does this mean that they are socially productive too? Yes, if you believe that society benefits because the product sold by the good-looking salesperson is somehow inherently better. No, if you think it is the same product regardless of who sells it. The cosmetics example would argue that beauty is not productive socially—the quality of the perfume or the makeover is the same regardless of the beauty of its seller. What about prostitution, movie-acting, or some other service? The item being "sold" is inherently different depending upon who is selling it, and both its private and its social value are enhanced by the looks of the person providing the service.

Beauty is clearly privately productive; but thinking about it this way, in some cases it might be viewed as socially productive too—as benefiting society as well as those who are fortunate enough to be born beautiful or the employers who obtain their services. It is reasonable to argue that some services offered by the beautiful are inherently different from those offered by the

ugly, and that society is better off by having the beautiful provide these services.

A fair conclusion is that the effect of beauty on earnings,
choice of occupation, and sales or profits is privately productive.
The answer to the question, "Lookism or productive beauty?" is
a clear YES! if we are talking about productivity at the level of
a person or company. In many cases our preferences against the
ugly are no different from our socially unproductive discrimination against minorities. Indeed, in those cases our discriminatory preferences are counterproductive. There is no gain to society; and by channeling ugly people into certain roles, society is
less efficient economically than it would be if people worked in
jobs that used their skills most efficiently, independent of their
looks. A simple calculation, analogous to ones economists have
made to measure the cost to society of discrimination against
African Americans, suggests that the loss in economic efficiency
due to lookism is equivalent to one-quarter of 1 percent of total
compensation of employees, about $20 billion in the United
States in 2009.[6] Not large, but not tiny.

In other cases, our preferences for beauty are preferences for
services that are inherently better than they would be if provided by the ugly. Human beauty in some of its activities is no
different from artistic beauty. It would be hard to argue that
Daniel Hamermesh singing "*La donna è mobile*" is as socially
productive as Luciano Pavarotti singing that aria. Musical ability is inherent and should be viewed as socially productive. It is
equally hard to argue that society would be as well off looking
at Daniel Hamermesh on the big screen performing as James
Bond as it is looking at Daniel Craig in the same role, even if
I could act as well as Craig. Some of what we might view as
lookism is also socially productive. These potential positive ef-

fects mean that the $20 billion calculation is an upper limit to the cost to American society of lookism.

To some extent our preferences for beauty are purely discriminatory—are no different from the distastes of citizens in the majority for buying from, working with, or employing workers in some minority group. This kind of discrimination benefits the discriminator, but it hurts society overall. To some extent, though, and in certain cases, our preferences for beauty represent tastes for ideals that enhance human well-being generally and that are socially productive. Which cases are which is hard to say; but most people, if they think about it, can identify individual cases, can view socially productive beauty the same way that Justice Stewart viewed pornography—and can "know it when [they] see it."

WHAT ARE THE SOURCES OF BEAUTY EFFECTS?

Regardless of the extent to which our preferences for beauty are socially productive or not, possibly simpler questions to answer are: (1) Whose behavior causes the beauty effects? As the discussion of the standard economic theory of discrimination made clear, preference-based discrimination could arise from the tastes of the employers themselves, from an individual's fellow workers, or from consumers of the products or services to whose production the worker contributes. (2) Is there any direct evidence—on the amount actually produced instead of dollars of sales revenue—that beauty is even privately productive?

Combining the effects of looks on sales, profits, and pay, you would infer that discrimination by consumers is most consistent with the evidence. If employers were at fault, and consumers didn't care about the looks of those selling to them, there could be no effect on sales. The same holds if fellow employees were the discriminators. But if consumers are discriminating, employers will profit by catering to their preferences, by hiring the beautiful and paying for the scarcity of beauty, thereby increasing sales and perhaps even profits.

The difficulty with this inference is that it is indirect—one would like something that identified the source of the discrimination more directly. If you could set up an experiment that would allow you to distinguish among these sources of the beauty premium, how would you do it? One possibility is to imagine a set of unexpected and naturally occurring disfiguring injuries that occur differentially across members of the labor force. Perhaps a plague randomly strikes adults, independent of their demographic or economic characteristics or any prior experiences that they might have had, and it renders their faces permanently and severely scarred. These disfigurements make some unfortunate workers worse-looking; and we can assume that some companies and some occupations had employed more of the disfigured workers than others. A simple test would compare wages before and not too long after the plague has struck in relation to the degree to which the workers have contact with customers. If the source of the pay difference is customer discrimination, you would expect to see a bigger drop in wages among those disfigured workers who have more customer contact.

Going still further with this same "natural experiment," how do the before-after pay differences vary with the number of fellow employees who work with the disfigured individuals? If, for example, you find that the suddenly disfigured workers who come into contact with many other employees in their company suffer larger wage declines than those who have few fellow workers (or, indeed, if the latter experience no change in wages), you can be pretty sure that the ugly worker's fellow employees are the source of the beauty effect in the labor market.

What if neither comparison, among workers whose jobs differ by the extent of customer contact, or among workers distinguished by the number of fellow employees, shows any difference in the before-after differences in earnings between disfigured workers and those who were more fortunate? Despite their absence, though, you observe that the typical disfigured worker has suffered a decline in earnings compared to those workers who were not disfigured. If that were the case, you would have to infer that the source of the beauty premium is the employer. You would conclude that employers just prefer to surround themselves with better-looking employees.

No such naturally occurring plague has occurred; and fortunately there has not even been a man-made disaster that has randomly disfigured enough workers to allow researchers to make the kinds of comparisons needed to isolate the sources of the beauty effect. Minor beautifying efforts, like better clothing, cosmetics, and beauty treatments, have little effect on how your beauty is perceived; but perhaps examining changes in the experience of people who have undergone major facial plastic surgery might allow deducing the paths by which beauty affects earnings?

There are two problems with considering the effects of plastic surgery on earnings. First, the number of uninjured workers undergoing major reconstructive surgery on their faces is minute. Second, it is very unlikely that those few who do obtain this kind of surgery are a random sample of all workers. Given that the surgery is elective, most beneficiaries have had above-average incomes beforehand and are in jobs where, so they believe, an improvement in their appearance might matter most. The treatment—major facial surgery—is far from what would be necessary to consider this a controlled experiment.

Absent a carefully controlled experiment, or any way of using information on major surgery, we cannot look at people before and after their looks have changed and hope to infer the causes of the beauty effect. This puts us at a disadvantage compared to a huge and still burgeoning literature in economics that has evaluated social and economic programs by examining outcomes before and after the program began among those people, geographic areas, or demographic groups who were or were not treated by the program. We are thrown back on non-experimental situations, where we compare people whose other characteristics that could affect the outcome of interest can be controlled to as great an extent as possible. This approach is clearly far from ideal; but it is the best that the real world offers us, absent unethical interventions that might, for example, allow us to disfigure some randomly chosen group of workers in order the conduct the necessary research.

WHAT IS THE DIRECT EVIDENCE ON THE SOURCES?

The best study to examine this question tried to circumvent the absence of data thrown up by real-world experiments by creating a laboratory experiment.[7] The researchers used Argentine university students, with some randomly designated as "employers," and with others randomly designated as "workers."

Each worker's photograph was rated on the usual 5 to 1 scale by a large number of high school students, as was each employer's photograph.

By giving different groups different treatments, the authors designed a way to infer how much of the beauty effect was due to preference-based discrimination and how much to payoffs to characteristics that could raise a worker's productivity. The "employment situation" was that each worker had to complete as many mazes as possible in a short period of time. The payoff was based on the number completed, on what the worker expected to complete based on a brief trial maze, and on what the employer expected that the worker would complete. By using the trial maze the researchers allowed for a correlation of beauty and self-confidence—based on the worker's estimate of his or her eventual "productivity" after the trial—and what the employer was willing to pay for completed mazes. These variations enabled the researchers to distinguish discrimination from differences arising from possible correlations among verbal self-confidence, employers' stereotyping, and productivity.

The main conclusion of the study was that the majority of the effect of beauty was not due to preference-based discrimination. Instead, much of the impact of beauty was through the channel of greater self-confidence on the workers' part and better verbal skills. The translation of these measures to the real-world analog of labor productivity may not be perfect; but the study does suggest that employers' treatment of bad-looking workers is not entirely unproductive socially.

In another laboratory study, researchers tried to discover whether more information about actual "productivity" was sufficient to modify the relationship between the amounts received by people and their beauty.[8] This was not designed to mimic the employment relationship. Instead, it was part of a well-known laboratory game, in which members of a group of people are given some money and told that, if they contribute $1 to the common pool, members of the group as a whole will receive money back totaling more than $1. To understand the game, ask yourself how much you would contribute to the pool if you were in a group with three average-looking strangers; then ask yourself how much with a group of three good-looking strangers; then with three of your closest friends.

Again using university students, the authors had other students rate the participants' looks (from photographs), this time on a 9 to 1 scale. Students who were rated as better-looking elicited larger contributions to their group's general pool than did other students. But after their fellow participants were told how much the better-looking students themselves had contributed to the general pool, they then contributed less than did participants in other groups that contained fewer good-looking participants. There appeared to be preference-based discrimination in favor of the good-looking students, but that favoritism was implicitly based on expectations that those students would be more "productive" for the society consisting of participants in this game. Once the good-looking students were shown to be no more socially productive than others, the beauty premium became a penalty.

Another study used a different kind of game to examine the same phenomenon. Each of a group of students was shown photos of a group of students from another university and asked how much money each would offer to each of the pictured individuals. A second group of students was shown the same photos and asked how much money they would insist on receiving from the pictured individuals.[9] Pictures were rated by yet a third group of students, this time on an 11 to 1 scale. Good-looking people were offered more money; but when students were responding to photos of good-looking students, they expected the good-lookers to offer more themselves. This study is consistent with the view that beauty is at least somewhat socially productive, so long as we are willing to make the giant leap from lab experiments to the real world.

Laboratory experiments allow researchers to isolate factors that would be difficult to adjust for statistically even with the best available data describing actual labor markets, or that for practical reasons simply could not be generated in the real world. They are increasingly popular research tools for economists. But my guess is that you are wondering whether they really tell us anything about behavior outside the laboratory—and your wonderment is well-founded. The analogy between the laboratory experiment and the real-world labor market is always imperfect—the games cannot be perfect reflections of employment relations. This makes it difficult, as the discussion here has shown, to translate laboratory results to inferences about behavior in real-world labor markets. Another difficulty is that the stakes of these games are generally much smaller than those in actual employment situations—in one study the average payoff was $3.84, infinitesimal compared to the $230,000 difference in lifetime earnings between the good-looking and the bad-looking in the United States. Also, the relationships are much shorter-lived. Finally, the participants in these experiments are almost always university students, hardly typical of real-world employers and workers.

While missing certain aspects of these nicely controlled laboratory environments, a structured game played by randomly chosen contestants can, if properly analyzed, provide some information about how beauty pays off in labor markets. It can, moreover, avoid some of the difficulties just noted, including the use of students as laboratory subjects. In a study of a Dutch television game show, British researchers tried to infer the relative importance of preferences for beauty from the contestants' behavior, and to test whether there was a causal relationship between beauty and social productivity.[10] Each game consisted of five contestants who answered questions posed by the moderator. In each of the first three rounds, the contestant who buzzed first would place part of his or her initial endowment of money and/or prior winnings in play, and receive that amount if the question was answered correctly, or forfeit it if not. After each of these rounds the person who did best in the round would choose a fellow contestant for elimination, with the person eliminated losing all of his or her winnings. In the final, fourth round, the two remaining contestants would play another game that based the payoffs on how much the two together (as a mini-society) had earned up to that point.

The authors had a large number of adults rate the contestants' beauty on a 7 to 1 scale based on photographs. The ratings were characterized by the same gender and age differences as usual—more dispersion among women, and lower average ratings of older players. The research questions were whether the decision of the winner of a round to eject a fellow contestant was related to the contestant's beauty, and whether the contestants' beauty was related to their productivity—to their ability to answer questions and thus increase the winnings of the group of contestants, the "society."

In each round the average beauty of those eliminated was less than that of the average player. As a result, the average beauty of the surviving players rose as the games progressed. The success of the bad-looking contestants in answering questions, however, was no less than that of the other contestants: There was no apparent relation between beauty and social productivity.

The greater success of better-looking contestants on the show was due entirely to their fellow contestants' preferences for good looks. Given the structure of the game, it is difficult to analogize the result to labor markets in order to infer whether it represents employer, employee, or customer discrimination. But the result strongly indicates the importance of tastes for beauty absent any relation between beauty and social productivity.

Even a television game show, one that involves substantial amounts of money, is very far removed from actual labor markets. We can learn a bit more about the sources of the beauty effect in actual labor markets by consulting the studies of beauty in specific occupations. Although we did not link them specifically to sources of beauty, they do tell us something about this topic. In the study of attorneys, for example, the fact that litigators were better-looking than transactional attorneys (those less likely to appear in front of a judge or jury) suggests the importance of customers' preferences.

Additional evidence from the study of attorneys makes this point more strongly. Good-looking attorneys who spent their early careers in the public sector, and who thus did not need to attract clients, were more likely than worse-looking public-sector attorneys to move to the private sector, where their looks might help them attract clients. Among attorneys in the private sector, the effect of good looks was greater on the earnings of those who were self-employed, who needed to obtain clients and did not have an employer, than on the earnings of attorneys who were employed in law firms. This last result in particular suggests that discrimination by employers, or by fellow employees, is a less important source of the beauty effect than discrimination by customers.

The studies of professors also suggest the importance of customer discrimination. After all, the students who are evaluating professors are customers in a very real sense. Since at least some small amount of pay in most universities is related to how well the instructor is appreciated by students, there is an indirect translation from customers' (students') higher instructional evaluations of good-looking faculty to their higher pay.

Additional, albeit anecdotal, evidence is provided by the complaints of some female tennis players in the 2009 Wimbledon tournament. During many of the tournament's rounds, Centre Court, the focus of fans' attention and the most likely to be shown on television, featured matches between players noted for their beauty as well as their tennis prowess. The BBC, which broadcast the tournament, denied being responsible for the assignment of players to Centre Court, but a spokesperson implicitly acknowledged the role of consumers' preferences when he noted, "It's advantageous to us if there are good-looking women players on Centre Court."[11]

Thinking about these examples illustrates the difficulty of inferring when beauty is socially productive. The tennis example seems to be the least likely: The quality of tennis is generally no better when provided by Maria Sharipova than by a less good-looking, equally able competitor, but sponsors might benefit from showing off Sharipova's beauty. The professors' example is tougher: Students may learn more because the good looks of the professor lead the student to attend class more frequently and, perhaps, pay more attention to the substance of the professor's lecture. The attorneys' example seems more difficult still. Certainly, if one side wins a civil suit because its attorney's better looks influenced the jury, the other side loses. Her beauty is privately but not socially productive. But, like the beautiful professor, if her looks also get the jury to pay more attention to her sensible arguments and render a fairer judgment, her beauty is also socially productive.

THE IMPORTANCE OF BEAUTY

Beauty matters in economic transactions because people care about the looks of those with whom they interact. Because *people* provide services and sell goods, their looks become part of the goods and services that customers buy. If you buy something from a bad-looking person, you are buying a product or service whose purchase makes you less happy and less willing to pay as much. Being ugly means being less productive to your employer in many jobs. Your lower productivity results from people discriminating against you—you are harmed by the prejudices of all of your fellows. Consumers' preferences for beauty discriminatorily appear to make bad-looking people less productive in the eyes of employers. But in some of these cases beauty is socially productive—it doesn't just raise sales, and perhaps profits; it also makes an arguably inherently better product or, more likely, an inherently better service.

So who causes the inferior treatment of bad-looking people in labor markets, the discriminatorily lower earnings that they receive, the lower productivity in the minds of their employers, and the occasional fillip to the inherent quality of what we consume? We all do. As suggested by the classic comic strip, *Pogo*, "We have met the enemy and he is us."

PART III

Beauty in Love, Loans, and Law

CHAPTER 7

Beauty in Markets for Friends, Family, and Funds

What good is beauty if nobody likes you?

—*Sign carried by street person, Austin, Texas, February 12, 2009*

BEYOND THE LABOR MARKET

Beauty matters in labor markets—and it surely also matters in an immense variety of non-economic activities. If you agree to spend time with friends, you are exchanging something with them—your time—and getting their time in return, even though no money is exchanged. Time is scarce, and each party could spend it with someone else—or alone; you have alternative uses of your time. Your choice means that you are giving up the opportunity to be with other people in favor of time spent with these friends. How beauty affects even this most rudimentary non-monetary exchange is an economic question, since the sharing involves your scarce time.

Much of what I discuss here has to do with matching—how groups of people form, how individuals match one-to-one with each other in dating and marriage, and how they obtain monetary preferment when they match with lenders. The marriage market is especially interesting and important. In most modern societies nothing other than token rings are exchanged. No dowry or bride price is paid. Yet a marriage implicitly involves the exchange of a promise of a lifetime spent together—doing things together and, most important for our purposes, looking at each other and sharing a gene pool to pass on to the next generation. These latter two considerations involve each spouse's looks, so in this most important of transactions, we should expect beauty to play an important role.

HOW IS BEAUTY EXCHANGED?

Exchanging beauty for non-economic returns is not that much different from exchanging beauty for pay at work. But there are a few differences, mostly because, unlike a job where it is just the worker's beauty that is being exchanged for money, here at least two parties are *both* exchanging their beauty with each other and exchanging beauty for their partner's other characteristics.

What would two-person partnerships look like if the only trait that people had was their beauty, everybody appraised human beauty the same way, and everybody valued beauty? The most beautiful person would be partnered with the next most beautiful, the third-most with the fourth-most, all the way down to a partnership between the ugliest and second-most ugly person. We saw that agreement about beauty is imperfect, so this set of pairs is an extreme case; but so long as there are common standards of beauty, as we know there are, better-looking people will tend to be matched with other better-looking people—there will be good-looking couples and bad-looking couples.

Beauty isn't the only thing people care about. What if there is another trait, say intelligence, that people value in their partners. In thinking about whom to partner with, I desire their beauty *and* their intelligence, and they want mine. Assume, as the evidence showed, that there is no correlation between beauty and intelligence—a woman supermodel is just as likely to be very bright or quite stupid, and so is a male superstar. In forming partnerships, so long as both traits are valued, those who are beautiful can use that desired characteristic to attract partners who have both beauty and intelligence to offer. Beautiful people will attract other beautiful people; but they will also be able to trade their beauty for a partner's intelligence. The outcome will be that beautiful people will be matched together; they will also be matched with people who are not so beautiful, but who instead can offer their intelligence in the exchange.

Intelligence is just one of many characteristics aside from beauty that people might desire in a partner. Others might be height, good health, education, family connections, a good name, and, no doubt, many others. The beautiful can exchange their beauty for these other desirable characteristics; and their ability to do so will lead to good-looking people being partnered with people who are themselves good-looking and who possess many of these other desired characteristics. Beauty will be associated with partner's beauty, and it will also be associated with partner's intelligence, education, family name, and other characteristics. Most generally, beauty will be associated with any partner's characteristic that brings more to the partnership, including the partner's ability to provide material things—his or her ability to earn money.

HOW DOES BEAUTY AFFECT
GROUP FORMATION?

This discussion has been totally general—it could apply to the formation of groups of people or to two-person relationships. It could apply to short-term relationships or to longer-term, even lifetime relationships. The general principles of exchange are the same in all of these cases, but there are specific differences that make each unique.

You start life off engaging with people you didn't choose, such as your parents and other older relatives. Even here beauty plays a part. Most babies are viewed as cute, and their perceived cuteness induces their parents and others to bond with them— to treat them better. By the time we start school, though, we must choose who to spend our scarce time with. Whom will we invite for play dates from among the choices in our pre-school class? Who will be our "best friend" in third grade? What social group will we sort into in middle school and high school? Even this last question misses the essential point: We do not usually sort into preexisting groups—we form groups with others. Middle school or high school groups are not like college sororities or fraternities that one attempts to join. They are formed anew based on individuals' preferences for being with one another, and for avoiding spending time outside the group.

Even after decades have passed, most of us remember from our high school years the particular groups to which we did or did not belong. If we have a good memory, we can even recall the names of classmates who belonged to the various groups. In Willowbrook High School in suburban Chicago, class of 1961, there were the athletes/cheerleaders (a group to which I most definitely did not belong), the intellectuals (my group), the "hoody" kids (a 1950s term denoting D.A. haircuts and

denims), and no doubt others. (These terms are extremely anti-
quated, and I leave it to the reader to discover what a D.A. haircut looked like and whence the appellation came.) The groups
were not rivals—these were not gangs. But we spent time mostly
with others in our group. The groups contained both boys and
girls, and typically even dating was within the group and in fact
helped to define the group.

Does beauty play a role in the formation of these and other
groups, and how does it affect their formation? Even though
beauty is just one characteristic that matters, if people value
the looks of others, they will value looks in choosing members
of a group to associate with. A better-looking group member
enhances the status of the group, creating pleasure for existing group members who get the chance to associate with her.
Perhaps at least as important, a better-looking group member
makes the entire group more attractive to outsiders. She makes
it easier for the group to attract more, and more desirable,
members. It benefits others, raising the value of group membership for everyone. The effect is the same as when a religious cult obtains another adherent, whose attendance makes
joint prayer more enjoyable for both existing and prospective
members.[1]

Social psychologists have created an immense literature examining the formation of groups, particularly among adoles-
cents. The issue is of particular interest in that age group, because then you have the freest choice about group adherence.
Earlier in life options are limited by the very small social circle
you have contact with. Later on you are concerned more with
one-to-one matching—dating and marriage—than with becoming part of a possibly larger group.

The psychologists' evidence, which typically considers many
factors and occasionally even beauty, is that group members

tend to resemble each other along a variety of dimensions, just as the general discussion predicted.[2] These dimensions include intelligence, athleticism, economic background (in those schools that do not obtain a student body from an already homogeneous population), ethnicity, and religion. The three groups from Willowbrook High School reflected exactly this kind of sorting.

Economists have tried to get at the role of beauty in group formation with experiments. Using non-student adults, economic experimenters examined how a group of Peruvians behaved when faced with incentives to contribute part of an initial endowment given by the researcher to a group fund, which in turn could pay back more than contributed to the initial amount. But that additional amount was paid out only when other group members contributed, with the total of the extra contributions split among the group's members.[3] In a final round of the game the participants were allowed to choose members of a group that they would want to belong to. People who were rated as better-looking by an independent panel of raters (who were not participants in the experiment) were more likely to be chosen to join a group. Beauty proved to be important in group formation, even after the authors adjusted for how much each participant had contributed in earlier rounds of the game.

HOW DOES BEAUTY AFFECT DATING?

Most of the interest in non-market exchange of beauty is in its role in two-person relationships. Aside from how widespread such relationships are and their importance for procreation, they have the additional advantage of being easy to analyze— we only need to consider two people's preferences and abilities, not three or more people's behavior. Gender differences are especially interesting here, with the crucial point perhaps captured in Sam Cooke's song, "Wonderful World":

Now I don't claim to be an "A" student
But I'm trying to be,
So maybe by being an "A" student baby
I can win your love for me.

This 1960 song, which has been used in movies (*Witness*) and is still heard in elevators today, expresses a set of common beliefs about the dating market: The man believes that the woman wants success (being an "A" student), while nothing is mentioned of her skills other than the man's implied infatuation, perhaps with her looks. The central question in this section is how beauty is exchanged in dating relationships—what each party is looking for, and how that differs by gender. That in turn lays the foundation for the more important question of the next section—how beauty is exchanged in creating a marriage.

There is nothing unique to *homo sapiens* in the potential for exchange of characteristics in dating and mating. Similar exchanges occur with variations in the animal world too. Assuming that the goal is to pass one's genes on to the next generation, each party would like to demonstrate reproductive fitness in the form of health and strength. Male dung beetles grow ever larger horns, whose display attracts females because the male can use his horns to defend the tunnels where the females will lay their eggs. One might view the male dung beetle's horns as analogous to the songwriter's desire to become an "A" student. Presumably the female dung beetle who seems healthiest (prettiest) will attract the male dung beetles with the largest horns, maximizing each party's chance of reproductive success.[4]

The possibility of exchange of characteristics, and beauty in particular, was made especially vivid for me in my introductory economics class when I asked students for examples of actions undertaken by others for their own gain but that affected the student indirectly. One described the following situation. Her roommate, who she said is very pretty, had a huge poster of her boyfriend over her bed, and every day my student had to look at it from her own bed. "Why did this poster impose a negative effect on you?" I asked. She answered, "The boyfriend is really ugly." After the uproar in the lecture hall subsided, I then asked why, if the roommate is so pretty, she dated this bad-looking guy. My student's answer was, "He goes to Harvard." There may be other reasons for the match; but perhaps the young gentleman was exchanging his earnings potential (under the assumption that his acceptance by Harvard signaled his earnings potential, or perhaps even that a Harvard education might make him more productive) for the roommate's good looks.

Social psychologists have long been interested in the determinants of dating preferences and matched dates, and a few have focused on the role of looks in this exchange.[5] Economists have recently gotten into this business too, and we have added some new twists to the research. The researchers have in some cases availed themselves of the immense amounts of data available from online dating sites, going far beyond small samples of student participants. Also, the preferences are placed into a framework of rationality and are inferred from actual behavior, not from expressions of what people might desire as elicited in surveys.

The role of scarcity and some hints about gender differences in the exchange of beauty are provided by a recent media controversy, popular music, and one of my favorite jokes. All illustrate how supply and demand interact to affect the chances of a match being made and the nature of what the parties exchange. The role of scarcity when there is an excess of women was suggested in 2008 by the mayor of a small North Queensland, Australia, town, who commented, "with five blokes to every girl, may I suggest that beauty-disadvantaged women should proceed to Mount Isa."[6]

The effect of a shortage of men is suggested by Jan and Dean's 1963 song "Surf City," which talked about boys going to Surf City because there were "two girls for every boy." At the other end of the life cycle, a woman stood up after dinner in an old-age facility and announced to the diners (among whom, as at most such residences, men were very scarce), "Whoever can guess what I'm holding behind my back can have sex with me tonight." One gentleman yelled out, "Elephant." The woman replied, "Close enough."

A recent study conducted at the University of North Carolina–Chapel Hill offers more than anecdote on this subject.[7] Using thirty coeducational Southern colleges, whose percentages of female students in 2006 ranged from 47 to 85, the author had students at her school rate the beauty of nearly 1,500 Facebook photographs of women on a 10 to 1 scale. The hypothesis was that competition for dates would lead to better-looking women attending schools where men were relatively scarce. This might arise if high school girls, being aware of conditions in different schools, sorted themselves in part by the sex ratio (the number of men per woman) at prospective colleges. Or it might occur because the college women, finding dates scarce, made special efforts to enhance their physical attractiveness, and these efforts showed up in their Facebook pictures.

As it turned out, the schools' sex ratios did affect the average looks of women at different colleges, but not quite as expected. Increases in the percentage of women up to 60 percent (well above the national average) were accompanied by increases in the average attractiveness of a campus's coeds. Above that, the beauty of the women decreased as the campus became even more heavily female. So there is some recognition by women of the role of looks in the dating exchange; but it is difficult to explain why, when men become especially scarce, the effect disappears. Perhaps with extremely low percentages of men the women just gave up; or perhaps pre-college sorting disappears at some very low sex ratios.

To examine the issue more closely, several economists have analyzed the results of speed-dating festivals, in which series of men and women are matched briefly and then asked whether they would be interested in pursuing the relationship further. One set of researchers created their own small-scale speed-dating events, in which several (9 to 21) graduate students spent a few minutes with each of a number of others of the opposite sex.[8] "Successful" outcomes occurred when participants asked for contact information on individuals whom they had met during the brief speed-dating encounters. Each respondent rated his/her own beauty before the event, and each had his/her beauty rated by others who participated in the event. Intelligence, taken as a characteristic that might be exchanged for beauty, was measured by the average SAT score of the student's undergraduate school.

The authors found gender differences in the effects of attractiveness and intelligence on the likelihood of a person's success with the opposite sex. Men put more weight on a woman's attractiveness, and women put more weight on a man's intelligence. These results are consistent with the belief that beauty matters more to men, and potential economic success matters more to women's dating choices. The gender differences in the responses, particularly to beauty, were not large, though: The responses of women to men's attractiveness were over four-fifths as big as men's responses to women's attractiveness. Beauty seemed to matter for both genders in this study.

A much broader study was conducted on the dating behavior of people who were involved in an Internet-based dating service.[9] Success was defined as occurring when one registrant sent an email seeking to contact another. Attractiveness was rated by groups of undergraduates based on photographs of the large number of registrants. The beauty measures thus correspond closely to best-practice standards for rating beauty.

Both men and women responded more positively to more attractive members of the opposite sex; but there was no evidence of any difference in the response by gender. Nor were better-looking men or women more likely to respond more or less strongly to better looks in the opposite sex. Despite this similarity between men and women in their responses to looks, the authors did observe that, as in most of the research, women's preferences for a man rise as his education level increases, but that this effect was not so strong in men's preferences for women. Relative to their valuations of beauty, women put more weight on characteristics that indicate an ability to earn more money.

HOW DOES BEAUTY AFFECT MARRIAGE?

The results from studies of dating are interesting and informative; but the expressions of preferences about dates, and even the actual choices of dates, reflect low-cost decisions. A bad date might cost you several hundred dollars and one unpleasant evening. Marital choices are not low-cost: They are expressions of preferences for a match that is expected to last for many years. These matches are usually not made without very careful consideration of their long-term costs and benefits. In most countries they involve huge investments of time and money even before the marriage occurs.

For most people the ultimate purpose of dating is marriage. Economists view dating and marriage as analogous to job search and long-term employment. Both dating and job search are ways of gathering information about prospective matches that, one hopes, will eventually lead to a match that is more or less permanent. The exchange of information about jobs is two-way: Employers learn about you. You learn what you like about jobs and also learn something about your real-world capabilities. Similarly, prospective mates, the people you date, discover what you are like in a relationship, and you discover what they are like— and more generally what your preferences are about prospective mates. The end result in most cases is a long-term match, of a worker with an employer, or of one spouse with another.[10]

Long-term marriages (and jobs) create surpluses for the partners. In both cases the match enables both parties to be better off than if the match had not been made. If that were not true, then the match would disappear. One party or both would initiate the end of the match—a worker would quit or be laid off, and the couple would divorce. The interesting economic questions in analyzing marriage are how large a surplus is created, and how the spouses share that marital surplus.

So long as a surplus can be created, it will be. In terms of the focus on beauty, this suggests that there is no reason to expect any difference in the likelihood of marriage as individuals' looks vary. So long as a prospective spouse, even a very unattractive one, can find someone to whom he or she can offer something advantageous along some other dimension(s)—intelligence, height, strength, sex appeal, family name, or whatever—a match will take place, as some marital surplus can be created.

Is this correct? Are bad-looking people as likely to be married as good-looking people? An old joke argues no:

> A woman walks into a store and purchases 1 small box of detergent, 1 bar of soap, 3 individual servings of yogurt and 2 oranges. The cashier says, "You must be single." She responds, "You can tell that by what I bought?" The cashier says, "No, you're ugly."

Seventy-two percent of the respondents in the two American data sets that underlay some of the analyses of chapter 3 were married. Among the above-average-looking people, it was 73 percent, and among the below-average, it was 69 percent. The differences by looks in the percentage married were not statistically significant. At least within the broad ranges of below-average, average, and above-average looks, this discussion describes behavior correctly. Bad-looking people are not much less likely than good-looking people to be married. The joke is funny, but wrong.

The exchange of beauty for a spouse's other characteristics is shown by data on own beauty and spouse's education from the American surveys collected in the 1970s and from data on Shanghai, China, from 1995. Except for the comparison of good-looking to average-looking wives in the United States, beauty has the expected effect on the education level of the spouse you have matched with. Below-average-looking individuals match with spouses with less education. In the American data this is especially true for women in the bottom 15 percent of looks: Their husbands have on average one less year of schooling than other husbands. A husband's bad looks are less strongly related to his wife's education.[11]

The effects are not small. The discussion of beauty in labor markets showed that an extra year of schooling is associated with about 10 percent extra earnings among men. As compared to an average-looking woman, a below-average-looking woman is married to a man who will bring about 11 percent less earnings into the household.[12] If men on average earn 50 percent more than women, this means that this is the same effect as her bad looks causing her to earn over 15 percent less than an average-looking woman.

Although measured differently, the Chinese results are very similar to those from the United States. Fifty-nine percent of above-average-looking wives have husbands with at least a high school diploma, while only 50 percent of average- or below-average-looking women do. As in the United States, the differences between their wives' education of men classified by looks are smaller. Again, education seems to be traded for looks; and it is men's education, in particular, which increases their earnings potential, that is traded for feminine beauty.

These calculations help to explain the apparent anomaly that the impact of bad looks on women's earnings appears to be smaller than on men's. We saw that bad-looking women are paid less than other women; and we have seen that they are not much less likely than their sisters to be married. Their major additional income disadvantage arises because the husbands they match with earn substantially less than the husbands of better-looking women. Good-looking women can trade their looks for a husband's better ability to provide, and bad-looking women can't.

Additional evidence of gender differences in the relative importance of looks and education is shown in a study of an online dating/marriage service in Korea. In addition to all the usual information, the service provided photos that were used to measure the participants' looks.[13] The comparisons showed that women were much less willing to reduce their requirements for additional education in a prospective mate than were men.

That the exchange of beauty for desirable characteristics tends to be quite one-sided is shown explicitly by matrimonial advertisements in Indian newspapers.[14] Women in a study of ads in one paper described themselves in three categories of looks. Men seeking brides wanted potential brides with at least above-average looks in over two-thirds of the ads. Women mentioned men's looks only rarely.

All of these findings demonstrate clearly what has long been celebrated in DuBose Heyward's song, "Summertime," from *Porgy and Bess*:

Oh, your daddy's rich
And your mamma's good lookin'
So hush little baby
Don't you cry.

Accepting the characterization of dating/matching as women trading looks for men's earnings potential, why does this particular set of valuations arise? What underlying conditions might expect us to observe this kind of trade? One could simply assert that men prefer looks more than do women, but that assertion is both ad hoc and sexist. But as long as full-time female workers earn less than full-time male workers, or even if people mistakenly believe this is so, it would pay women to trade off their looks for men's earnings capacity when these matches are made.

What if women had the same earnings capacity as men, everybody knew that there is equality of potential earnings, and there was no gender discrimination in labor markets? Would we still observe this trade-off in marital matching? The answer is yes. Even when workers' skills and their preferences for beauty are identical by gender, it is still possible for a social norm to persist that leads one gender (men) to trade off their earnings power for the other gender's (women's) looks. A society can remain in a world where gender differences in the trade-off of beauty for earnings exist long after gender differences in earnings have disappeared.[15]

I have dealt with the trade-offs within marriage that are created by the spouses' looks. But what about the looks themselves? The theory predicted that good-looking husbands will have good-looking wives, and vice-versa. Is this true in reality—are spouses sorted along the dimension of beauty?

Psychologists have examined this issue for many years, with results that have repeatedly demonstrated that better-looking men tend to be married to better-looking women. Most of these studies have taken a few couples, have had outside observers rate the looks of the spouses based on photographs, and have shown that there is a positive relation between the ratings of wives and their husbands.[16] Other studies have asked raters to match photos of men and women—to guess which ones are married to each other—with the result that, because the raters assumed that good-looking people match to each other, their guesses were far more accurate than if they had picked randomly.[17]

To examine couples' looks on a larger sample, take the data on the Shanghainese households from 1995. These are the only data I am aware of on a broad sample of households in which both husbands' and wives' looks were rated. With random matching, we would expect only 12 percent of couples to contain both a good-looking husband and wife; but in fact 25 percent of couples contained two good-looking spouses. We would expect only 45 percent of the couples to have both partners average or below-average in looks, not the 58 percent that occurred.[18] Couples sort even along the single dimension of looks, just as we expected.

COULD THERE BE A MARKET FOR BEAUTIFUL CHILDREN?

Beauty can be exchanged for money and other characteristics today, and today's exchange can produce long-term benefits, perhaps reaching into future generations. Indeed, today's exchange of beauty can link generations. It is illegal to sell your children—you cannot produce a child and then shop around for buyers. What if, however, you could choose your child's beauty, or at least have some influence over it beyond yours and your spouse's genetic endowments? This is not a nightmare out of *Brave New World*. We are not yet able to decant Alphas upon demand. It is perfectly legal and possible, though, for a couple in which fertilization cannot occur, but implantation of a fertilized ovum can, to obtain a donated ovum that was fertilized in vitro by the husband's sperm.

If you seek unfertilized ova you may take what you can get—you may not be able to choose how good-looking the donor is. Although it apparently never materialized, an attempt at commercializing the sale of ova to generate better-looking children appeared on the Internet in the early 2000s. The owner of the website was trying to create an auction of the ova of a set of models whose photographs were displayed, and advertised:

> Many men have substantial financial resources, yet are unable to find the genetic combinations that would impart beauty to their offspring. . . . If you could increase the chance of reproducing beautiful children, and thus giving them an advantage in society, would you? Any gift such as beauty, intelligence, or social skills, will help your children in their quest for happiness and success.[19]

The owner recognized that beauty and money can be exchanged outside labor markets, and was attempting to profit from creating a market that would stimulate this kind of exchange.

The idea of this auction is appalling, but it does allow an interesting exercise. What would be the price of an auctioned ovum produced by one of these women? How much should a couple be willing to pay for one of the auctioned ova? The website listed starting bids between $15,000 and $150,000. Do these prices reflect what sensible people should be willing to pay in the open market?

The calculation of an appropriate price in some ways resembles the calculations in chapter 3 of the lost earnings that resulted from facial disfigurement, except here we are talking about the gains to beauty rather than the losses arising from impaired looks. Presumably the child who results from the auction of ova will, as the advertisement suggests, have "an advantage in society." The child will be able to earn more during adulthood; but since earnings typically do not materialize until at least nineteen years after fertilization, the extra benefits of beauty occur far into the future and must be discounted back to the present. The outcome for the child depends on what the child would earn without the fillip to beauty that is perhaps made possible by the purchased ovum.

Thinking about the genetics of procreation, we know that half the genes will come from the father and will be the same regardless of the choice of the egg donor. The question is whether a child's looks can be inferred by the casual observer as a combination of the father's looks and that of a random egg donor, or whether they will be expressed in ways not visible from the biological parents' physiognomies. This is an impossible question to answer, one that is linked to the general question of heritability. While many people believe that parental expressions of such traits as longevity, height, and intelligence are fully heritable, this is not true.[20] Randomness plays an important role in all of these outcomes. If this is also true for looks, but we assume that looks are fully heritable, we will over-estimate the value of a purchased ovum.

Let's assume that the model is in the upper 10 percent of looks. The largest possible economic gain, which would occur if looks are fully heritable, if the child would eventually obtain a graduate degree, and if a randomly chosen ovum donor would have been in the bottom 15 percent of looks, is $105,000. Even this, the best gain one could hope for from this auction, is below the top amount listed as the starting bid. If you obtain as much pleasure from your children's economic well-being as your own, paying more than $105,000 is justified only if there is a substantial non-economic value of producing unusually good-looking children. No couple should pay a huge amount for an ovum donated by a gorgeous model merely for the possibility of producing a child whose possible good looks might offer economic advantages later in life.

The same calculations could be made if we were to imagine a commercial sperm bank that would charge different prices to couples with an infertile husband depending on the looks of the sperm donor. Prices at sperm banks are currently very low: One leading bank charges around $500 per vial of sperm.[21] The maximum prices that a buyer should be willing to pay are, as these calculations show, substantially above that. My guess is that this kind of differential pricing hasn't yet appeared in the sperm bank market because the ready supply of potential donors keeps prices so low.

DOES BEAUTY MATTER WHEN YOU BORROW?

One of the best *Saturday Night Live* skits was Eddie Murphy's "White Like Eddie."[22] The comedian masquerades as a white man and goes to a bank to get a loan. When the African American assistant leaves, Eddie is told by the bank vice president that he can have as much money as he wants, can re-pay the loan whenever he wants, or simply not re-pay it at all. This skit underscores a crucial and much-debated issue in personal finance—whether and to what extent ethnic/racial minorities are discriminated against in credit markets.[23] While there is no skit to illustrate this possibility for beauty instead of race, one wonders whether credit markets treat beauty the same way as Eddie Murphy suggests they treat race.

Why might an applicant's beauty affect success in obtaining credit? The possible reasons are the same that might affect success in labor markets. Lenders might take bad looks as a signal that the person is a poor credit risk—bad looks might signal negative characteristics that are good predictors of a person's likelihood of defaulting on a loan. In that sense, poor outcomes for bad-looking applicants would indicate statistical discrimination. Another possibility is the pure preference-based discrimination that characterizes customers' attitudes and gives rise to the penalties that bad-looking workers experience in labor markets.

A large online lending market, Prosper.com, provides information on whether a loan was granted and its terms, the interest rate obtained, the person's demographic characteristics, and a photograph. Three recent studies have used these data to determine whether looks matter in loan markets.[24] The most relevant found that above-average-looking borrowers were more likely to obtain loans, even with the same demographic characteristics and credit histories as worse-looking applicants. They also paid lower rates of interest on their loans than other borrowers. This is a near-perfect reflection of the "White Like Eddie" phenomenon. But despite getting better terms on their loans, the better-looking applicants were more likely to be delinquent on those loans. So beauty was a very poor predictor of performance, suggesting that lenders were not using beauty as a device to infer something about potential borrowers, but rather that they simply preferred dealing with better-looking borrowers.

This discussion of credit markets illustrates yet another area where a person's beauty modifies an economic exchange. Research in this area is just beginning, and the evidence is very far from conclusive. It does seem, though, that lenders are willing to exchange more generous terms on loans for the pleasure of dealing with good-looking borrowers. They do this not because good looks predict that the loan will perform better, but because they are prejudiced against bad-looking applicants. They exhibit the same preference-based discrimination that appears to exist society-wide and that finds expression in a variety of other markets.

TRADING BEAUTY IN UNEXPECTED PLACES

Much of the focus of economists is justifiably on income and its determinants, because people derive much of their happiness from consuming what they have used their incomes to purchase. But we also derive much of our happiness from the pleasures that we obtain in non-monetary exchanges. We get some of these pleasures because of our good looks—or we fail to get them because our looks are somehow deficient. Our looks buy us friendship and economic support from our peers; and, especially for women, they buy economic support from a spouse. The difference between the genders in markets for matching with prospective marital partners is striking. Men are more concerned with women's looks, women more concerned with other aspects of the prospective partner, including his ability to generate an income. The 2009 movie *The Ugly Truth* advertised the central relationship by showing the female lead holding a heart next to her head and the male lead holding one over his pants.

Our behavior allows us to monetize our looks—to trade our beauty for non-monetary benefits that in turn have some monetary value. It enhances the economic importance of looks beyond areas that are obviously economic. Put more bluntly, the epigraph to this chapter has got it exactly wrong: Yet one more reason why beauty pays is that it induces more people to like you.

CHAPTER 8

Legal Protection for the Ugly

FAIRNESS AND PUBLIC POLICY

Fair is not a word that economists use a lot. We are more concerned with how people's characteristics affect market outcomes, predicting the effects of changes on those outcomes, examining incentives, and so on, than with asking whether an outcome meets some criterion of fairness. But having demonstrated that there is a beauty premium, and an ugliness penalty, in so many areas of daily life, it is worth asking the question: Is it fair that some people, who happen to be born and grow up bad-looking, are disadvantaged in so many ways compared to others who are, for examples, no more intelligent, strong, or physically fit?

Most industrialized societies have instituted policies designed to protect disadvantaged citizens in a variety of areas. These include labor markets, housing markets, and access to public facilities. At the federal level in the United States, protected groups include racial, ethnic, and religious minorities; women; older citizens; and disabled citizens. Most other industrialized countries have similar protections. In some countries and some American states and localities, protection is also provided based on sexual orientation. The question here is whether it would make sense to offer similar help to what one journalist I talked with called the "looks-challenged" citizen—perhaps the 10–15 percent of citizens whose looks are considered by their peers to be below average, or perhaps only the 1–2 percent who are considered homely.

One can easily imagine policies that would offer bad-looking people protections similar to those now offered to other disadvantaged citizens. Are there good arguments for providing these protections? Do the potential benefits outweigh the potential costs? That there are likely to be benefits seems certain, since proposed policies in any area almost always confer some benefit on at least some people. Whether other citizens might be disadvantaged by those policies—whether the policies generate unintended negative consequences for society as a whole—is always a more difficult question to answer. But it needs to be addressed when any policy proposal is presented. That is especially true in the case of beauty, given the novelty of the idea of protecting this particular group.

WHAT KINDS OF PROTECTION ARE POSSIBLE?

Before delving into specific existing policies that might be used to protect the ugly, it is worth discussing the more general policies that have been enacted to aid certain "protected classes." In the United States, these classes of citizen are typically helped by two types of policy. The first is legislation—be it federal, state, or local—that explicitly mandates protecting specific groups of people in certain specified activities. The second is through government purchasing, again at all levels of government, through which protected groups must receive certain types of preferences in employment by government contractors.

Many states had long had anti-discrimination laws covering various groups, particularly minorities, before legislative protection at the federal level began with the Equal Pay Act (EPA) of 1963. The EPA required employers to offer female and male employees the same pay if they were performing "equal work on jobs the performance of which requires equal skill, effort and responsibility, and which are performed under similar working conditions" within an establishment. This legislation outlawed gender discrimination in employment, fairly narrowly defined, within companies engaged in interstate commerce.

State laws were to a large extent superseded by the passage of the Civil Rights Act of 1964, whose Title VII prohibited employment discrimination based on the now well-known protected categories of "race, color, religion, sex or national origin." These protections were to be overseen by the Equal Employment Opportunity Commission (EEOC). Its purview soon came to include the protection of workers ages forty and up under the Age Discrimination in Employment Act (ADEA) of 1967. In 1990, Title I of the Americans with Disabilities Act (ADA) added "qualified individuals with disabilities" to the list of protected groups.

The ADA would seem to be the most obvious existing vehicle at the federal level through which to offer generalized protection to bad-looking workers. Its Section 12102 defines disability as "a physical or mental impairment that substantially limits one or more major life activities," with the latter term defined as including, "caring for oneself, performing manual

tasks, seeing, hearing, eating, sleeping, walking, standing, lift-
ing, bending." None of these limitations appears to apply to the
bad-looking—the language would seem to exclude the ugly.
But the section goes on to define disability to include people
"regarded as having such an impairment," defined as existing "if
the individual establishes that he or she has been subjected to
an action prohibited . . . whether or not the impairment limits
or is perceived to limit a major life activity." One might argue
that bad looks could be included under this latter extension of
the definition of disability and thus that the ugly are already
protected by the ADA.

All of these protections are aimed at labor markets. In 1968,
Title VIII was added to the Civil Rights Act to offer renters
and buyers explicit protections in housing markets. Over the
years it has been expanded to define as protected the same
characteristics that are covered by the panoply of federal anti-
discrimination laws covering employment. With state and local
analogs to the federal legislation, there is a ready-made vehicle
for protecting the ugly in other areas, including lending markets, where they are also disadvantaged.

The other possible general avenue for protecting the ugly
is affirmative action, first introduced by President Kennedy
under Executive Order 10925 in 1961, and linked to federal
contracting by President Johnson in 1965 under Executive Order 11246. The idea was to use the federal government's role as
a purchaser of goods and services, and as a provider of subsi-
dies, to induce employers to adopt and implement policies that
would aid protected groups. In areas such as hiring, promotion,
access to education and others, the program, monitored by an
office in the U.S. Department of Labor, requires employers to
file "affirmative action plans." These must show past progress

and promises of additional efforts to meet stated "goals and timetables" for future progress in enhancing opportunities for racial and ethnic minorities and for women.

Nearly fifty years after its inception, affirmative action remains highly controversial, to the point that there is not even much agreement on whether it has been beneficial on net for the groups it has been aimed at, much less about its overall desirability. Affirmative action would hardly seem to be an ideal vehicle to which to attach still additional protections, but it could be used. One could include the bad-looking as another protected class, requiring an employer to offer plans that would indicate how homely people would be hired into entry- and upper-level positions, advance up job ladders, etc., in order to achieve goals describing their eventual position in the company.

Numerous states and localities have enacted protections that extend federal legislation to some of the relatively few companies that are not covered by federal laws because of their size or line of business. Many have created state or local affirmative action programs, essentially mandating compliance by those companies and organizations that do business with the state or local government. These sub-federal extensions become binding, and are most relevant for this chapter, where they include additional groups that are not subsumed under federal protections.

Michigan and San Francisco have laws that expand protection to include weight and height explicitly. The City of San Francisco Human Rights Commission, which monitors the treatment of members of an unusually large variety of protected groups, describes its task as:

> The investigation . . . [and mediation of] complaints of discrimination in employment by businesses . . . based

on a person's race, color, creed, religion, national origin, ancestry, age, sex, sexual orientation, gender identity, domestic partner status, marital status, disability or AIDS/HIV status, weight and height.[1]

The local legislation does not explicitly protect against discrimination based on looks, but it would not be a large step to add this additional group to those already covered.

In a very few jurisdictions, that protection does exist. These include Santa Cruz, California; Urbana, Illinois; Madison, Wisconsin; and Howard County, Maryland.[2] Most recently, the District of Columbia has enacted fairly broad protections for employees, by making it illegal "to discriminate . . . on the basis of outward appearance for purposes of recruitment, hiring, or promotion" (Section 512 of Title 4—Human Rights— of the DC Municipal Code). In another section, protection is offered on the basis of personal appearance in rental housing, mortgage lending, and numerous other aspects of housing markets. These are the only jurisdictions that as of 2008 had legislated explicit protection in employment based on appearance independent of height or weight. The state of California does, though, prohibit discrimination in housing on the basis of "personal characteristics, such as a person's physical appearance . . . that are not related to the responsibilities of a tenant."[3]

One of the broadest-based legislative protections based on looks can be found in France. Its labor code states:

> Concerning recruitment; access to a placement or in-company training program; pay; training; redeployment within a company; posting; qualifications; job classification; promotion; transfer from one workplace to another;

and renewal of contract, provides that no person can be eliminated due to their ... physical appearance.[4]

This provision offers an extremely broad protection to employees, although the code makes it clear that the initial burden of proof is borne by the employee.

HOW HAVE EXISTING POLICIES BEEN USED?

Even under federal, state, or local legislation that does not explicitly protect bad looks in labor, housing, or other markets, a substantial number of lawsuits have been brought seeking case-law protection for people based on their looks.[5] Many of them have linked some aspect of appearance to existing protections based on their race, gender, or religion. For example, in *Hollins v. Atlantic*, 188 F.3d 652 (6th Cir. 1999), an African American woman claimed racial discrimination on grounds that a policy concerning hairstyles applied only to her. Her claim was rejected. Two men argued that their employer's preventing them from wearing earrings constituted sex discrimination (*Kleinsorge v. Island Corp.*, 81 F.E.P. Cases (BNA) 1601 (E.D. Pa. 2000)). Their claim was denied, with the court arguing that gender differences in standards of appearance are permissible. In *Swartzentruber v. Gunite Corp.*, 83 F.E.P. Cases (BNA) 181 (N.D. Ind. 2000), the plaintiff argued that his firing for having a tattoo depicting a Klansman with a burning cross violated protections of his religious beliefs. His claim too was rejected.

Courts have been unwilling to include appearance, as manifested in dress or decoration, as a protected expression of racial, religious, or gender identity. The treatment of appearance, as manifested in weight, is a different story.[6] A number of successful claims have been brought under EEO (Equal Employment Opportunity) protections, for example, *Frank v. United Airlines*, 216 F.3d 845 (9th Cir. 2000), with female flight attendants arguing that weight restrictions were applied differently by gender. Most weight cases, however, have been brought under the ADA, with the argument typically being that obesity, or even overweight, is itself a disability. A plaintiff who simply asks for ADA protection for being overweight, without claiming it is a disability, does not generally obtain relief (e.g., *Coleman v. Georgia Power Co.*, 81 F. Supp. 2d 1365 (N.D. Ga. 2000)). If, however, a plaintiff can demonstrate morbid obesity, to the point where it restricts a "major life activity," the person can receive relief—have the disability accommodated by the employer—under the ADA (*Cook v. Rhode Island Department of Mental Health, Retardation, and Hospitals*, 10 F.3d 17 (1st Cir. 1993)).

While successful ADA cases have involved claims that morbid obesity qualifies as a disability, a number of cases have been brought under the ADA and other statutes that have argued for protection based on claims that bad looks alone constitute a disability. In 2003, the EEOC sued McDonald's on behalf of an employee who had a port wine stain covering much of her face. In another case, a manager refused to fire a Kentucky Fried Chicken counter worker whom he had hired and who was missing his front teeth, which the manager's own supervisor found potentially offensive to customers. The district and circuit courts ruled for KFC, arguing that the absence of front teeth hardly limited a major life activity. Nonetheless, it seems a fairly small stretch to argue, based on all the evidence in this book, that reduced earnings are a limitation produced by this kind of disfigurement and consistent with the ADA.[7]

The case law in the jurisdictions that explicitly ban discrimination based on looks is extremely sparse. In a case brought under the District of Columbia code in 2008 (*Ivey v. District of
Columbia*) that is still in the courts, the Appeals Court reversed
the case's dismissal by the trial court and allowed some of the
plaintiff's claims to be re-heard. Ivey, a local bureaucrat, argued
that her supervisor "told her she would do a better job if she
were more attractive . . . and that he would like her better if she
looked like her attractive coworker." The case is not over, but it
is nearly unique in that the argument is based mostly on physical appearance, not gender and not weight nor even looks as a
disability. As such, it could illustrate the paths by which a broad
expansion of protection for the bad-looking might occur.

IS IT POSSIBLE TO PROTECT THE UGLY?

There are two questions that need to be discussed in order to
address this issue. Viewing protection for a group of individuals
as a benefit that is supplied by society: (1) Could we even agree
on which people are sufficiently bad-looking as to merit protection under some policy designed to aid this particular group? In
other words, can there be agreement among those who might
supply protection under legislative or other provisions about
who should be protected, given the inherent subjectivity of
views of beauty? (2) Would those people who we agree should
be the focus of protection ever be willing to come forward and
demand its protection? In other words, would those who might
potentially wish to be helped under laws or administrative provisions be motivated to seek help—to ask for redress from the
courts if necessary?

The first question would require some legislature, executive agency, judge, or jury to agree on what constitutes denial of a right because people's looks are sufficiently below the average to have singled them out for disparate treatment. Observers do not agree perfectly on what constitutes bad (or good) looks, or on what is sufficiently far below-average as to constitute ugliness. One attorney commenting on this issue claimed:

> Efforts to ban discrimination against employees based on their "personal appearance" are even more problematic. While height and weight can be measured, a person's overall appearance cannot. There is, by definition, a profoundly subjective element to the inquiry. What attributes, for example, should be considered in determining one's personal appearance?[8]

People's views of beauty are subjective; but the evidence has made it abundantly clear that people's views are highly correlated. Somebody who is viewed as unusually ugly by one observer tends to be viewed the same way by most other people. While subjective, perceptions of beauty are far from random. A person's beauty can be measured.

There will undoubtedly be disagreements by the suppliers of protection about exactly who is to be protected, but those do not seem insurmountable. The issue is not as simple as determining who might possibly be subject to gender discrimination—by and large that is a yes-no issue. These disagreements are qualitatively no different, though, from disagreements over the extent to which somebody who has some African American ancestry might qualify for protection under various anti-discrimination laws. That particular issue has arisen in a variety of cases. While I find its discussion repugnant, reminiscent of the racial laws in Nazi Germany, it has been dealt with and must be considered if we wish to protect this particular class.[9] The dividing line between those who might be included in this kind of class and those who would not is as arbitrary as it is in distinguishing on the basis of looks. It has been surmounted in those cases, and could be handled in lawsuits brought on the basis of discrimination against the ugly.

Would there be any demand for protection? Would people be willing to admit that they are bad-looking if there were some forum for obtaining compensation for the disadvantages that their looks have caused them? Without having tested the demand for protection by a newly entitled class, we cannot be certain that offering protection would elicit that demand. But the history of cases under the ADA offers some guidance on this issue. The ADA was enacted in 1990, and the EEOC did not start enforcing it until July 1992. By 1997, the EEOC was receiving over 20,000 cases per year under the ADA.[10] Disability may be a more clear-cut issue than bad looks, but even that is not obvious. Organizations such as the Body Image Task Force have as their stated goal fighting against prejudice based on physical appearance and would, I believe, be happy to help organize plaintiffs to take advantage if legislative protection of the ugly were instituted.[11]

I have shown that bad looks can generate an earnings disadvantage of perhaps $140,000 over a lifetime compared to the earnings of an average-looking worker. Add to this amount reasonable punitive damages, and there is a clear monetary incentive for an individual to sue his or her current employer, or even a prospective employer in the case of hiring discrimination. With an incentive amounting to more than three years of earnings, I doubt that people will be unwilling to acknowledge their bad looks.

Legal action takes money—the cost of filing and pursuing a legal case based on looks would probably far exceed the likely recovery from a lawsuit brought by a single individual. Just as in the case of suits claiming discrimination based on gender, race, or ethnicity, though, one can imagine that trial lawyers will seek to form classes of individuals and pursue class-action lawsuits. Obtaining certification of a class spreads the cost of bringing the lawsuit over enough plaintiffs to make the recovery sufficient to attract class members—and to make it potentially worthwhile for plaintiffs' attorneys to pursue legal action on their behalf. Class certification is often quite difficult, so that of all the pitfalls that might stand in the way of this extension of protection to bad-looking individuals, this might be the most severe. But with a large enough class, and with the potential for large recoveries for each person, these lawsuits will be filed.

In 2005, a class of ethnic/racial minorities and women who argued that promotions were offered disproportionately to white men sued Abercrombie and Fitch. The retailer agreed to a settlement of $40 million with members of the class. Since then individual employees have alleged that the company rates potential sales workers on their looks and offers existing workers more opportunities if managers rate them higher on a scale of "hotness."[12] The aggrieved individuals acknowledge that they have no current legal recourse. But you might infer from their current claims that, if they did, they would have no qualms about taking advantage of it.

When people are willing to supply a good or service, and others demand it, if governments don't intervene to prohibit the exchange, some price will be established, either in a visible market or implicitly, and exchange will take place. As yet there is no generalized formal protection for bad-looking individuals in labor and other markets. Governments implicitly limit lawsuits based on claims of looks discrimination. The potential supply of and demand for legal protection is there, but exchange is not allowed. But what if it were—if legal protection were explicitly granted to below-average-looking individuals? The returns to protection, indicated by the probability of those cases succeeding and the amounts recovered in successful cases, would be demonstrated over time through the case law and would determine the number of cases that people would file. A market of sorts for looks-based lawsuits is waiting to be born.

WHAT JUSTIFIES PROTECTING THE UGLY?

Imagine the following book: It starts off by showing that a particular group of people has a characteristic that remains essentially unchanged over their lifetimes unless they incur huge expenditures to alter it artificially. That characteristic makes its members less likely than other citizens to be working for pay and earning money. When they do work for pay, members of the group earn less than other workers, even after adjusting for the amount and kind of education that they have obtained and for numerous other earnings-enhancing characteristics. When they marry, the education and thus the earnings ability of their spouses is less than that of others' spouses. Companies that employ members of this group do not generate as much sales revenue as others. The group's members typically date and marry other group members. Finally, members of the group occasionally sue and recover for deficiencies in their earnings.

I have essentially described this book, with the group being below-average-looking individuals. Yet if I had substituted
African Americans, the discussion would, with minor changes,
have been very much the same. Changing race is very difficult.
The employment rate of African Americans—the fraction
of the population working for pay—is less than that of non-
Hispanic whites, and that is especially true among men. Sixty-
six percent of non-Hispanic white males were employed in
2008, but only 57 percent of African American adult males
were. Among women, the discrepancy is in the same direction
but is much smaller, 54 percent to 53 percent.[13] Given the level
of education of African American men, their earnings are about
20 percent lower than those of non-Hispanic white men, with
the difference among women being nearly 10 percent.[14] Indeed,
African American men's earnings disadvantage, adjusted for
the earnings-enhancing characteristics that they bring to labor
markets, is similar to the disadvantage experienced by below-
average compared to above-average-looking male workers generally. While not much attention has been paid to the issue, the
research that has looked at it suggests that an African American adds less to his or her company's revenue than does a non-
Hispanic white.[15] Since their educational attainment is lower,
and they generally marry other African Americans, the educational attainment of their spouses is less than that of the spouse
of a typical non-Hispanic white.[16]

In short, every specific research result about beauty could,
with some alterations, apply to African Americans. In discussing apparently discriminatory outcomes that harm African
Americans, I believe the same problem exists about the ultimate
source of their disadvantage: Employers appear to discriminate,
but do their actions simply result from their preferences against

African Americans, or is it that they are the proximate agents of harm because their customers prefer not to deal with African Americans? No doubt some of the apparently discriminatory outcomes experienced by African Americans result from employers' exercising their own preferences; and certainly much of the thrust of public policy has targeted employers. But much also results from customers' refusal to deal with African Americans without the equivalent of a monetary bribe.[17]

The situation of African Americans is obviously much different historically from that of bad-looking people. But the current similarities in the situations of the two groups may provide as much logical justification for protecting ugly workers through public policy as for protecting African Americans. In both cases—among African Americans and among bad-looking workers—the negative outcomes that occur in many markets are the result of the preferences that the majority has imposed on those markets. If we protect one group whose disadvantages arise from those preferences, why not protect the other? On economic grounds the arguments for protection seem the same for both.

With the exception of the discussion of dating and marriage, the same arguments could be made if we were to replace bad-looking citizens, or African Americans, with women. Given their level of education (on average identical to men's in the United States), their earnings are lower, with the earnings disadvantage being about 15 percent after numerous adjustments for other determinants of earnings.[18] Companies that employ otherwise identical women have lower sales, and so on.[19] While there obviously is no inherent prejudice by customers against women generally, the most useful theory of discrimination that underlies studies of the disadvantages that women face in various markets is based on societal views about women's roles. One can readily interpret those views as reflecting consumers' preferences—the same as the sources of the apparent discrimination against the ugly.

WHAT JUSTIFIES NOT PROTECTING THE UGLY?

The arguments in favor of protection seem very powerful. A leading legal scholar has argued passionately on fairness grounds that legal protections should be extended to bad-looking people and that those protections should be enforced vigorously.[20] Why not? After all, absent any logical basis for distinguishing among groups to be protected, why should members of one group benefit from government aid while others whose situations seem similar do not? The only possible arguments against protection must be based on the potential harm done to other groups by adding protections for the group proposed here—the bad-looking. Otherwise, protecting the bad-looking would seem likely to benefit society overall.

One might argue that the average citizen—a representative of the majority—is harmed when an additional group of disadvantaged citizens is protected. To the extent that the labor of the two groups is substitutable in employment, additional protections for the ugly would reduce wage rates and/or lower employment opportunities for better-looking workers, particularly those who just miss qualifying for protection—the near-ugly, in this case. Even if protection of the ugly doesn't affect others' employment opportunities, such protection would still require the majority to pay taxes to finance the bureaucracy that would enforce any regulations. While correct, this objection could be raised against the protections afforded to any minority group. Indeed, because the disadvantages experienced by protected groups are produced by the preferences of the majority behaving as consumers, members of the majority are precisely those who should be made to bear the costs of protecting the minorities whom they have disadvantaged.

If the costs of protection are only to be borne by the majority whose preferences generate the disadvantages for the ugly, what could be the argument against granting preferences for bad-looking workers in the labor, housing, and other markets? One possibility is that lookism is so socially productive that to enforce legal protections against it would reduce its social productivity. It is socially productive; but I doubt that the social productivity of preferences for good looks is sufficient to overcome their economic costs. And, even if it did, the fairness issue arguably would trump any concerns about social productivity.

There is another argument, also based on fairness, that seems much stronger. Considering as interested groups only majority citizens and bad-looking citizens leaves out all the other non-majority groups that are currently offered legal protection. The crucial economic issue here is the extent to which offering protection for bad-looking workers might reduce the labor-market and other opportunities of minority and other citizens whom we might choose to aid through legislation and regulation.

There is no evidence on the degree to which employers are able to substitute bad-looking for minority workers, and thus on the extent of job or earnings losses that minority and other protected workers might experience if special preferences were granted to ugly workers. A few studies, though, have examined whether workers in one disadvantaged group—for example, low-skilled African Americans—tend to be substituted for or against by workers in other disadvantaged groups—for example, low-skilled Hispanics.[21] The evidence is not dispositive, but it does suggest that employers tend to treat as substitutes workers in different low-skilled and disadvantaged groups, including some of those which are protected by U.S. policy.

Put in stark terms, aiding workers in one disadvantaged group tends to reduce wages and take jobs away from those in other disadvantaged groups. What if the same phenomenon characterizes how employers treat bad-looking workers compared to other disadvantaged workers? We would then have to infer that offering protection to bad-looking workers would harm workers who we have already determined deserve protection, and who already receive it through legislation and regulations.

What if this economic argument is incorrect, so that helping bad-looking workers does not cause economic harm to other disadvantaged workers? We would still have to make the political decision to spend scarce political resources—legislative action and regulatory and administrative effort and money—to the benefit of one group instead of another. Unless you believe that political will and administrative budgets are unlimited, which hardly seems likely, aiding the bad-looking means offering less aid to other groups which we currently protect or might wish to protect in the future. Public funds and energy are not unlimited. Even if different deserving groups are not economic substitutes, they are likely to be political substitutes—aiding one will reduce the amount of effort devoted to aiding another. And that substitution will produce economic harm to members of other disadvantaged groups, as the amount of aid offered to them is reduced by competition from the aid to the bad-looking.

WHAT IS THE APPROPRIATE POLICY?

The causes of mistreatment of the bad-looking, and their re-sults—inferior outcomes in a large variety of areas—seem little different either qualitatively or quantitatively from the mistreatment of other groups. Those include other minorities, be they racial, religious, or ethnic, and even a gender majority. In all instances one can argue that the disadvantaged group is harmed by the majority of citizens, or the most powerful citizens, who, for whatever reason, would prefer to deal with people who are more like themselves than deal with those in the disadvantaged group.

In the end, the decision about whether to aid bad-looking citizens in labor markets, housing markets, and elsewhere must be political. It has to weigh the relative merits of different groups that might be competing for help. Each group arguably has the same kind of economic claim on the sympathies of the majority, as the disadvantages of each have been generated by their inability to alter the characteristics that the preferences of the majority treat as inferior. Since some substitution, perhaps economic but surely political, exists between bad-looking and other disadvantaged groups, each of us has to make a value judgment about how deserving different groups are. Those views need to be translated into policy—or not—through the political process.

Judgments about this issue depend on how large a weight you put on the demonstrable gain in fairness that would come from protecting the bad-looking compared to the potential impacts on other, currently protected groups. On these considerations, the centrality of race in American history and the politics of the past sixty years suggest that we need to pay special attention to any potential reduction in protections for African

Americans when we contemplate offering additional protection to bad-looking Americans.

Regarding other protected groups, the concerns are less clear. Like the bad-looking, women and some ethnic minorities have an essentially immutable characteristic with which they were born. While religion is not immutable, American attitudes toward religious freedom suggest that the ease of changing your religion should not detract from arguments for its protection. Also, ethnicity, religion, and gender have been protected by federal law for nearly a half century. If we believe that there is either economic or political substitution of protection for one group against protection for another, concerns about these groups should make us think even harder about extending protection to the ugly.

Our willingness to protect disabled workers, embodied in the Americans with Disabilities Act, is the most recent extension of the protections offered at the federal level. Protection could be extended to include bad looks as a disability with a slightly broader interpretation of the ADA, one that goes beyond a basis in limitations on daily activities. This might be more acceptable if only the very worst-looking people, people who are generally agreed to be "1's"—including those with explicit facial disfigurements, either congenital or acquired—were protected. Whether protecting even this narrowly defined group is desirable is a less difficult question, but still one that requires thinking about the costs to groups that are currently protected.

The difficulties in considering this extension are illustrated in stark terms by the following example. Compare a person, now released from prison, who lost both legs in an automobile accident that was caused by his drunken driving and that killed another driver, and another person who has been unusually bad-looking since birth. Under current interpretations of the ADA, the disabled drunk driver must be offered accommodation in employment and other areas, but the bad-looking person will receive no such protection. This comparison leaves one wondering what the appropriate policy might be. I would argue in favor of protecting the ugly person rather than the drunk driver; but I would also realize that to do so would mean creating a set of rules that might reduce protection for disabled individuals generally.

Extending protection to the bad-looking in hiring and promotions in labor markets, and in access to rentals and to mortgages in housing markets, may be worth consideration. Bad-looking people should command the sympathy of others along a sensible Rawlsian criterion—essentially, there but for the grace of God go I, and that possible "I" deserves protection. Yet the ugly are only one of many groups of individuals who are deserving of protection. The scarcity of political energy for offering protection, and the distinct possibility that protected groups are substitutes in employment, should be considered seriously before we add the bad-looking to the list.

PROTECTING THE UGLY IN THE NEAR FUTURE

I would not be surprised if bad-looking Americans are eventually included among those citizens protected by anti-discrimination and related legislation. This extension would be especially likely if the definition of bad looks were kept very narrow. This might come in the form of an expansion from the small number of jurisdictions that have enacted legislation to protect the ugly to many more local and even state protections, and perhaps even to federal legislation. More likely, it could come through an expansion of protections under the case law, particularly under the ADA. But given how willing America has been to expand protection to additional groups since the first broad-based legislation was enacted, predicting the inclusion of the bad-looking under legal protection is a reasonable bet.

PART IV

The Future of Looks

CHAPTER 9

Prospects for the Looks-Challenged

THE BEAUTY CONUNDRUM

Beauty pervades specific aspects of economic behavior. But does it affect how we feel about our lives generally? Will the impacts of beauty continue over the near and even the more distant future that should concern all of us? At least as important, **should** beauty continue to matter: Does any evolutionary basis for our continued preoccupation with people's looks remain? What could we as a society do to lessen the negative impacts of bad looks on people's lives? If we do nothing and if the impacts of beauty do not disappear, what can looks-challenged individuals do to help themselves?

ARE BEAUTIFUL PEOPLE HAPPIER?

Ugly people earn less than average-looking people; and average-looking people earn less than the beautiful. Ugly people find entry into certain occupations more difficult; and if they choose those occupations, their earnings are penalized. Bad looks even affect our choices about whether or not to work for pay. Being bad-looking means you enter the dating and marriage game with a "weaker hand"—less to trade for the characteristics that you seek in a partner. You have less of a chance to obtain loans for housing and other durables.

So what? These are specific considerations. They involve how well people fare in particular aspects of their lives, including their work lives, their lives as consumers, and their family lives. What if, taking all these specifics together, beautiful people are no happier than average-looking or even ugly people? One could even imagine a "Richard Cory" phenomenon where, despite all these superficial advantages, beautiful people are actually unhappier than others.[1]

This is just not so; quite the contrary. Beautiful people are also happier than their less good-looking counterparts. Two of the surveys used in this book contain information on both beauty and happiness—people's responses to questions like, "How satisfied are you with life as a whole?" Fifty-five percent of the people in the top one-third of looks stated that they were very satisfied or satisfied with their lives; 53 percent of people in the middle half of looks said the same thing; but only 45 percent of the worst-looking one-sixth of the population said they were satisfied.[2] Bad looks and unhappiness with life go together; and that is especially true for people who most others would view as homely. Taken together, the negative effects of bad looks on a panoply of specific economic and social outcomes reduce people's overall happiness. As Dorothy Parker said, "Beauty is only skin deep, but ugly goes clean to the bone."

That unhappiness and bad looks are related is probably not surprising. What might be surprising is that the relationship is just as strong for men as for women.[3] The discrimination against ugliness and the favoritism toward beauty that characterize modern societies are not at all a gender issue; they are an issue facing both men and women.

WHAT WILL BE BEAUTIFUL?
WHAT SHOULD BE?

Perhaps the importance of differences in human beauty that produce all these negative impacts will decline in the future. After all, fewer and fewer people are disfigured. And, while our beauty is difficult to change, with increasing incomes and improved surgical and other technologies, maybe people's looks will improve on average. If so, perhaps we will pay less attention to what will have become less obvious differences in people's looks.

One author noted, "There's no reason for us to think that beautiful people are good and ugly people evil, yet we do."[4] Although we still view beauty as a signal of desirability in a potential mate, worker, or borrower, its continued use for these purposes does not seem justified. In rich societies today, beauty and health—reproductive fitness—are not generally correlated, although there may exist a minuscule minority of individuals whose bad health is signaled by bad looks. The evolutionary basis for the role of beauty in various markets no longer effectively exists.[5]

A recent study offers a glimpse of change.[6] Women in a wide range of countries were shown pictures of men's faces, all of which matched the symmetry standards of beauty, but which differed in their degree of masculinity (jaw line, nose size, and other aspects). The study showed that where people are generally healthier, women pay less attention to the degree of masculinity in a man's face. It suggested that as we get richer, our criteria about human beauty might change. But will they change to the point that we don't care about looks any more?

Perhaps; but even if distinctions among people's beauty become finer, it may be your beauty relative to others' that determines your payoffs. Given people's remarkable willingness and ability to make narrow distinctions among themselves, it is quite possible, with an increase in average beauty and greater homogeneity in looks, that the penalty for being just slightly worse-looking than other people might increase over time.

We cannot know what future standards might be, but people have implicitly speculated on them. One example is contained in the science-fiction series *Flash Gordon*, originally a comic-book series in the 1930s. Flash "lived" in the thirty-third century CE, and, along with his love interest, Dale Arden, has been depicted often over the past three-quarters of a century. As depicted in the original comic books from the 1930s, Flash was blond, squared-jawed, and mid-American. In the 2007 television series the actor who played Flash was again blond, square-jawed, and mid-American. The forward-looking depictions have been remarkably constant over these seventy-five years. In both cases the individuals qualify as being above-average in looks. Now their looks may be determined by the artists' or producers' desire to appeal to the standards of beauty held by potential contemporary (with the artist, not with Flash and Dale!) readers or viewers. But to some extent they can be viewed as predictions about what might be beautiful in the future. Taken as such, and to the extent that forecasting beauty standards is possible, they suggest that we believe that what constitutes human beauty is unlikely to change any time soon.

Taking all these considerations together, I doubt that our perceptions of human beauty will diminish in importance in our lifetimes. Industrialized societies are stuck in a low-level equilibrium. Our behavior is a relic of a set of responses that now lack a biological basis. In other areas of economic life, there are numerous examples of low-level equilibria that were established as a result of some past characteristics and that remain in existence long after underlying conditions have changed.[7] So too with beauty: the beautiful will be advantaged, the ugly will be disadvantaged, for many years to come.

WHAT CAN SOCIETY DO?

Even if some forms of protection for some bad-looking workers eventually come about, either through new legislation or new case law, most bad-looking workers will not find protection. Perhaps only the very worst-looking, those with severe disfigurements, might be helped. If that happened, people might feel that enough had been done and that the relevant problems had been solved. Yet the disadvantages of bad looks not only impinge on the worst-looking 1 or 2 percent of the population, but also on the one-sixth to one-eighth whose looks are viewed as below-average. The harm that most bad-looking people suffer will not be removed by legislation or lawsuits that protect a tiny minority. Without legal protection, what would eliminate the discrimination that the rest of society imposes on its bad-looking members in so many areas of life?

One solution is to try to keep unemployment as low as possible. We know that employers cannot afford to indulge consumers' preferences for workers' beauty at a time when labor is generally scarce. Aside from being desirable on macroeconomic grounds, a policy of the lowest possible unemployment would create the additional benefit of reducing the earnings disadvantage of bad-looking workers; and it might even spill over to their treatment in other areas.

Discussions of low-level equilibria in other contexts—addiction to cigarettes is a good example—suggest that maintaining a policy that temporarily moves a system far away from an undesirable equilibrium can alter the nature of the system.[8] Even if underlying conditions revert to the status quo ex ante, the system may not revert to the detrimental outcome if the changed conditions have been maintained long enough. Low unemployment and the resulting reduction in the disadvantages in employment opportunities experienced by bad-looking workers might, if they prevailed long enough, accustom consumers to deal with bad-looking people in different contexts and reduce underlying prejudices against them. Obviously, low unemployment and tight labor markets are unlikely to persist indefinitely; but they are generally socially desirable, and their potential beneficial impacts on bad-looking citizens offer one more basis for them.

WHAT CAN YOU DO IF YOU'RE BAD-LOOKING?

Persistent low unemployment that induces employers and customers to deal equally with people regardless of their looks is not likely to be sufficient to remove or even greatly reduce the disadvantages that bad-looking citizens experience in so many endeavors. It is also not likely that legislation or administrative actions will be broad enough to help most bad-looking citizens.

A social solution, be it imposed or evolutionary, is unlikely to solve most of the problems of the looks-challenged.

In the end, a bad-looking person will continue to face the question of how to adjust to societal discrimination in work, dating, and marriage, choice of housing, and other areas. The burden will, as it always has been, be on bad-looking people to make the most of their advantages and to minimize the impacts of the disadvantages caused by their looks. Substituting "less intelligent" or "uncoordinated" for bad-looking, this is the same prescription that you would offer people who experience disadvantages arising from their diminished intellectual ability or lack of athleticism.

In my media appearances discussing beauty I often get questions like, "If somebody is bad-looking, is there any hope for them in the labor market?" The answer is no and yes. No, in the sense that the research that I have presented makes it clear that bad-looking people generally do worse in a wide range of areas of daily life. I have presented evidence on many of these; and I have no doubt that there are others that I have not discussed where the same kinds of disadvantages will be demonstrated by future research.

The answer would be yes, though, in the sense that looks are only one of the many appealing characteristics that people possess. As the title of an advice article in a magazine for middle-aged women suggests, "Make the Most of Your Looks."[9] If I am bad-looking, I will avoid occupations (movie actor?) where my bad looks will penalize me greatly. Instead, I will choose an occupation where the skills that I possess in abundance have a chance to bring me the biggest rewards, both monetary and non-monetary, and where the rewards for the good looks that I lack are less important. So yes, plain people are penalized; but they can and should structure their careers to avoid the worst effects of those penalties. Remember, too, that although differences in beauty have large impacts, they account for only small parts of the differences in outcomes that people experience at work.

Similarly, in dating and marriage looks do matter initially. As the Beatles sang, "Would you believe in a love at first sight? Yes I'm certain that it happens all the time" ("With a Little Help from My Friends"). But most bad-looking people have other characteristics that can give them a romantic advantage that, with careful nurturing, can help remove the initial disadvantages that their physiognomies inflict on them. One could make the same arguments about credit and other markets. In the end, bad looks hurt us and will continue to hurt us. Looks are fate; but so are many other things. But bad looks are not a crucial disadvantage, not something that our own actions cannot at least partly overcome, and not something whose burden should be so overwhelming as to crush our spirit.

CHAPTER ONE: THE *ECONOMICS* OF BEAUTY

[1] The data on the time inputs are from the *American Time Use Survey*, 2003, category t6_10201. There were 5,240 married men in the sample, 5,763 married women, and 1,087 single women age seventy or over.

[2] From the Consumer Expenditure Survey, as reported in http://www.bls.gov/cex/csxstnd.htm#2008, table 3.

[3] Calculated by the author from the 1991–92 *Zeitbudgeterhebung*. The category is zh031, "*waschen oder anziehen*."

[4] *International Herald-Tribune*, August 13, 2008.

[5] Nancy Etcoff, *Survival of the Prettiest: The Science of Beauty* (New York: Doubleday, 1999); Naomi Wolf, *The Beauty Myth: How Images of Beauty Are Used Against Women* (New York: Anchor Books, 1992).

[6] *Vogue*, September 2009; *Men's Health*, December 2008.

[7] Timur Kuran and Edward McCaffery, "Expanding Discrimination Research: Beyond Ethnicity and to the Web," *Social Science Quarterly* 85 (September 2004), pp. 713–30.

[8] Daniel Hamermesh, "An Economic Theory of Suicide," *Journal of Political Economy* 82 (January/February 1974), pp. 83–98; Mark Duggan and Steven Levitt, "Winning Isn't Everything: Corruption in Sumo Wrestling," *American Economic Review* 92 (December 2002), pp. 1594–1605; Jeff Biddle and Daniel Hamermesh, "Sleep and the Allocation of Time," *Journal of Political Economy* 98 (October 1990), pp. 922–43; Lena Edlund and Evelyn Korn, "A Theory of Prostitution," *Journal of Political Economy* 110 (February 2002), pp. 181–214.

[9] One of the best non-economic analyses of beauty and its role in human behavior is by my colleague David Buss, *The Evolution of Desire: Strategies of Human Mating* (New York: Basic Books, 1994).

CHAPTER TWO: IN THE EYE OF THE BEHOLDER

[1] http://www.merriam-webster.com/dictionary/.

[2] Own translation of Bernhard Schlink, *Selbs Betrug* (Zürich: Diogenes, 1994), p. 9.

[3] *The New Yorker*, August 30, 2010, p. 36.

[4] http://news.bbc.co.uk/2/hi/africa/3429903.stm.

[5] In 2008, its GDP per capita ranked it 143rd out of 180 countries studied by the International Monetary Fund: http://en.wikipedia.org/wiki/List_of_countries_by_GDP_(PPP)_per_capita.

[6] *Genesis*, 29:17.

[7] Angus Campbell, Philip Converse, and Willard Rodgers, *Quality of American Life, 1971*. Available from Inter-university Consortium for Political and Social Research, Study No. 3508. Robert Quinn and Graham Staines, *Quality of Employment Survey, 1977*. Available from ICPSR, Study No. 7689.

[8] Daniel Hamermesh and Amy Parker, "Beauty in the Classroom: Instructors' Pulchritude and Putative Pedagogical Productivity," *Economics of Education Review* 24 (August 2005), pp. 369–76.

[9] Daniel Hamermesh, "Changing Looks and Changing Discrimination: The Beauty of Economists," *Economics Letters* 93 (2006), pp. 405–12. In a two-way analysis of variance of the standardized average looks ratings and the economists' identification numbers, less than one-third of the variance was within individuals.

[10] Formal statistical testing of the independence of the ratings within each pair sharply rejects the hypothesis that the ratings are random. The chi-square statistics are all highly significantly different from zero.

[11] From a two-way analysis of variance of the 5-point looks ratings and the interviewer numbers.

[12] All of the differences by age are significant statistically.

[13] Nancy Etcoff, *Survival of the Prettiest*, 1999.

[14] Elaine Hatfield and Susan Sprecher, *Mirror, Mirror . . .* (Albany: State University of New York Press, 1986), p. 283.

[15] Judith Langlois, Jean Ritter, Lori Roggman, and Lesley Vaughn, "Facial Diversity and Infant Preferences for Attractive Faces," *Developmental Psychology* 27 (January 1991), pp. 79–84; Judith Langlois and Lori Roggman, "Attractive Faces Are Only Average," *Psychological Science* 1 (March 1990), pp. 115–21.

[16] American Society of Plastic Surgeons, *2008 Report of the 2007 Statistics of the National Clearinghouse of Plastic Surgery Statistics*. Arlington Heights, IL: ASPS, 2008.

[17] www.cosmeticsurgerybible.com/2008/news/uk-tops-table-for-european-cosmetic-surgery-spending.

[18] Soohyung Lee and Keunkwan Ryu, "Returns to Plastic Surgery in Marriage and Labor Markets," unpublished paper, University of Maryland–College Park, 2009.

[19] The relatively small effects are based on calculations that account for differences in the women's family incomes and ability to spend. To the extent that the data allow, problems of endogeneity in the determination of spending on beauty have been accounted for.

[20] For China, see http://www.chinadaily.com.cn/english/doc/2004-07/05/content_345598.htm. Stories about the United States abound, for example, http://www.msnbc.msn.com/id/30112465/ and *More*, April 2009, p. 78.

CHAPTER THREE: BEAUTY AND THE WORKER

[1] The 10 percent figure comes from a multivariate regression estimated over a large random sample of Americans in 2007 (from the Current Population Survey, Merged Outgoing Rotation Groups). The true figure is probably much higher for the gains from finishing high school, or from finishing college.

[2] Author's calculations from Current Population Survey (ibid.).

[3] In 2009, men accounted for 52.5 percent of employees. Using that figure, these calculations are based on weighted averages of the beauty effects listed in table 3.1.

[4] Jeff Biddle and Daniel Hamermesh, "Beauty, Productivity and Discrimination: Lawyers' Looks and Lucre," *Journal of Labor Economics* 16 (January 1998), pp. 172–201.

[5] Andrew Leigh and Jeff Borland, "Unpacking the Beauty Premium: Is It Looks or Ego?" unpublished paper, Australian National University, 2007; Daniel Hamermesh and Jeff Biddle, "Beauty in the Labor Market," *American Economic Review* 84 (December 1994), pp. 1174–94; Daniel Hamermesh, Xin Meng, and Junsen Zhang, "Dress for Success—Does Primping Pay?" *Labour Economics* 9 (October 2002), pp. 361–73; Soohyung Lee and Keunkwan Ryu, "Returns to Plastic Surgery in Marriage and Labor Markets," unpublished paper, University of Maryland–College Park, 2009; Barry Harper, "Beauty, Stature and the Labor Market: A British Cohort Study," *Oxford Bulletin of Economics and Statistics* 62 (December 2000), pp. 771–800.

[6] Jason Fletcher, "Beauty vs. Brains: Early Labor Market Outcomes of High School Graduates," *Economics Letters* 105 (December 2009), pp. 321–25.

[7] At the very least, there are more claims of discrimination by workers when the unemployment rate is higher: John Donohue and Peter Siegelman, "Law and Macroeconomics: Employment Discrimination over the Business Cycle," *University of Southern California Law Review* 66 (March 1993), pp. 709–45.

[8] Philip Robins, Michael French, and Jenny Homer, "Non-Cognitive Traits and Labor Market Earnings of Young Adults," unpublished paper, University of Miami, 2009.

[9] Fletcher, "Beauty vs. Brains."

[10] Susan Averett and Sanders Korenman, "The Economic Reality of the Beauty Myth," *Journal of Human Resources* 31 (Spring 1996), pp. 304–30. John Cawley, "The Impact of Obesity on Wages," *Journal of Human Resources* 39 (Spring 2004), pp. 451–74; Christian Gregory and Christopher Ruhm, "Where Does the Wage Penalty Bite?" in *Economic Aspects of Obesity*, ed. Michael Grossman and Naci Mocan (Chicago: University of Chicago Press, 2011). Giorgio Brunello and Béatrice d'Hombres, "Does Body Weight Affect Wages: Evidence from Europe," *Economics and Human Biology* 5 (March 2007), pp. 1–19.

[11] Nicola Persico, Andrew Postlewaite, and Dan Silverman, "The Effect of Adolescent Experience on Labor Market Outcomes: The Case of Height," *Journal of Political Economy* 112 (October 2004), pp. 1019–53. Wenshu Gao and Russell Smyth, "Health, Human Capital, Height and Wages in China," *Journal of Development Studies* 46 (2010), 466–84.

[12] Dan-Olof Rooth, "Obesity, Attractiveness, and Differential Treatment in Hiring," *Journal of Human Resources* 44 (Fall 2009), pp. 710–35.

[13] *Wall Street Journal*, Friday-Saturday, November 26–27, 1993, page 1, quoting indirectly Naomi Wolf, author of *The Beauty Myth*.

[14] The quote, as it appears in various places, is "Es ist leichter ein Atom zu spalten, als ein Vorurteil."

[15] Compare, for example, the surveys of empirical evidence by John Pencavel, and by James Heckman and Mark Killingsworth, in Orley Ashenfelter and Richard Layard, eds., *Handbook of Labor Economics, Vol. 1* (Amsterdam: North-Holland, 1986); and the survey by Richard Blundell and Thomas MaCurdy in Ashenfelter and David Card, eds., *Handbook of Labor Economics, Vol. 3A* (Amsterdam: North-Holland, 1999).

[16] Arthur Goldsmith, Darrick Hamilton, and William Darity, "From Dark to Light: Skin Color and Wages among African-Americans," *Journal of Human Resources* 42 (Fall 2007), pp. 701–38.

CHAPTER FOUR: BEAUTY IN SPECIFIC OCCUPATIONS

[1] In the case of opera, the career of the soprano Florence Foster Jenkins early in the twentieth century provides the exception that proves the rule.

[2] The tabloids of the time referred to Hamlin and one other attorney on the show as "*L.A. Law* hunks."

[3] The late Zvi Griliches of Harvard University, personal conversation some time in the 1980s.

[4] Jeff Biddle and Daniel Hamermesh, "Beauty, Productivity and Discrimination: Lawyers' Looks and Lucre," *Journal of Labor Economics* 16 (January 1998), pp. 172–201. The twenty-four underlying categories were combined into four groups by an experienced attorney—my wife.

[5] Abigail Pogrebin, *Stars of David* (New York: Broadway Books, 2005), p. 10.

[6] http://news.bbc.co.uk/2/hi/europe/7581039.stm.

[7] Lee Lillard, "The Market for Sex: Street Prostitution in Los Angeles," unpublished paper, RAND Corporation, 1995.

[8] Paul Gertler, Manisha Shah, and Stefano Bertozzi, "Risky Business: The Market for Unprotected Commercial Sex," *Journal of Political Economy* 113 (June 2005), pp. 518–50.

[9] Raj Arunachalam and Manisha Shah, "The Prostitute's Allure: The Return to Beauty in Commercial Sex Work," unpublished paper, University of Michigan, 2009.

[10] www.theeroticreview.com offers detailed information for members on the characteristics of a huge number of escorts, along with prices charged for various services.

[11] Lena Edlund, Joseph Engelberg, and Christopher Parsons, "The Wages of Sin," unpublished paper, University of North Carolina–Chapel Hill, 2009.

[12] Mike Murphy, quoted by Maureen Dowd, *New York Times*, July 29, 2009.

[13] Daniel Benjamin and Jesse Shapiro, "Thin-Slice Forecasts of Gubernatorial Elections," *Review of Economics and Statistics* 91 (August 2009), pp. 523–36.

[14] Andrew Leigh and Tirta Susilo, "Is Voting Skin-deep? Estimating the Effect of Candidate Ballot Photographs on Election Outcomes," *Journal of Economic Psychology* 30 (February 2009), pp. 61–70.

[15] Amy King and Andrew Leigh, "Beautiful Politicians," *Kyklos* 62 (November 2009), pp. 579–93.

[16] Markus Klein and Ulrich Rosar, "Physische Attraktivität und Wahlerfolg: Eine Empirische Analyse am Beispiel der Wahlkreiskandidaten bei der Bundestagswahl 2002," *Politische Vierteljahresheft* 46 (2005), pp. 266–90.

[17] Niclas Berggren, Henrik Jordahl, and Panu Poutvaara, "The Looks of a Winner: Beauty and Electoral Success," *Journal of Public Economics* 94 (February 2010), pp. 8–15; Cheng-Da Li and Ming-Ching Luoh, "Beauty Premiums in Politics—The Case of the 2004 Legislator Elections in Taiwan," *Taiwan Economic Review* 36 (March 2008), pp. 67–113.

[18] Marcus Maurer and Harald Schoen, "Der Medial Attraktivitätsbonus: Wie die Physische Attraktivität von Wahlkreiskandidaten die Medienberichterstattung in Wahlkämpfen Beinflusst," *Kölner Zeitschrift für Soziologie und Sozialpsychologie* 62 (June 2010), pp. 277–95.

[19] Irene Frieze, Josephine Olson, and June Russell, "Attractiveness and Income for Men and Women in Management," *Journal of Applied Social Psychology* 21 (July 1991), pp. 1039–57.

[20] Anindya Sen, Marcel Voia, and Frances Woolley, "The Effect of Hotness on Pay and Productivity," unpublished paper, Carleton University, October 2010.

[21] Statistical evidence in favor of the notion that teaching quality affects salary is offered by William J. Moore, Robert Newman, and Geoffrey Turnbull, "Do Academic Salaries Decline with Seniority?" *Journal of Labor Economics* 16 (April 1998), pp. 352–66, who demonstrate the link between receipt of teaching awards and salary. The evidence on the impact of teaching evaluations is less direct, but my personal experiences in evaluating young faculty for tenure and teaching awards suggest that evaluations receive a lot, perhaps even too much attention in these processes.

[22] Daniel Hamermesh and Amy Parker, "Beauty in the Classroom: Instructors' Pulchritude and Putative Pedagogical Productivity," *Economics of Education Review* 24 (August 2005), pp. 369–76.

[23] Bernd Süssmuth, "Beauty in the Classroom: Are German Students Less Blinded?" *Applied Economics* 38 (February 2006), pp. 231–38.

[24] Daniel Hamermesh, "Changing Looks and Changing Discrimination: The Beauty of Economists," *Economics Letters* 93 (December 2006), pp. 405–12.

[25] David Berri, Rob Simmons, Jennifer van Gilder, and Lisle O'Neill, "What Does It Mean to Find the Face of the Franchise?" unpublished paper, Southern Utah University, 2009.

[26] Naci Mocan and Erdal Tekin, "Ugly Criminals," *Review of Economics and Statistics* 92 (February 2010), pp. 15–30.

CHAPTER FIVE: BEAUTY AND THE EMPLOYER

[1] Andrea Weber and Christine Zuhlehner, "Female Hires and the Success of Start-up Firms," *American Economic Association, Papers and Proceedings* 100 (May 2010), pp. 358–61.

[2] Quoted in an interview reported at http://www.telegraph .co.uk/fashion/3302299/You-can-always-get-what-you-want .html.

[3] Gerard Pfann, Jeff Biddle, Ciska Bosman, and Daniel Hamermesh, "Business Success and Businesses' Beauty Capital," *Economics Letters* 67 (May 2000), pp. 201–7.

[4] *De Tijd*, July 28, 2000, p. 32.

[5] Craig Landry, Andreas Lange, John List, Michael Price, and Nicholas Rupp, "Toward an Understanding of the Economics of Charity: Evidence from a Field Experiment," *Quarterly Journal of Economics* 121 (May 2006), pp. 747–82.

[6] Michael Price, "Fund-Raising Success and a Solicitor's Beauty Capital: Do Blondes Raise More Funds?" *Economics Letters* 100 (September 2008), pp. 351–54.

[7] Peter Kuhn and Kailing Shen, "Employers' Preferences for Gender, Age, Height and Beauty: Direct Evidence," unpublished paper, University of California–Santa Barbara, 2009.

[8] Reported in *Austin American-Statesman*, July 19, 2004, p. A1. A story in a Chinese newspaper in 2005 (in Mandarin) even reported that one government agency posted a help-wanted advertisement suggesting that only women with large breasts need apply.

[9] This difference has been shown for various years for many northern European countries by numerous authors, with one of the clearest demonstrations being by Dan Devroye and Richard Freeman, "Does Inequality in Skills Explain Inequality in Earnings Across Advanced Countries?" National Bureau of Economic Research, Working Paper No. 8140, February 2001.

[10] See, for example, George Borjas, *Labor Economics*, 4th edition (New York: McGraw-Hill, 2008), pp. 277–79, for a discussion of the idea of firm-specific human capital, a concept that goes back to the early 1960s.

[11] *Cash* 8, no. 34 (August 23, 1996), p. 1.

[12] Nicholas Rule and Nalini Ambady, "The Face of Success: Inferences from Chief Executive Officers' Appearance Predict Company Profits," *Psychological Science* 19 (2008), pp. 109–11.

[13] For the relationship between pay and company profits, see Kevin J. Murphy, "Executive Compensation," in *Handbook of Labor Economics*, vol. 3B, ed. Orley Ashenfelter and David Card (Amsterdam: Elsevier, 1999), pp. 2485–2563.

CHAPTER SIX: LOOKISM OR PRODUCTIVE BEAUTY, AND WHY?

[1] Merriam-Webster Online Dictionary, http://www.merriam-webster.com/dictionary.

[2] Gary Becker, *The Economics of Discrimination* (Chicago: University of Chicago Press, 1957).

[3] Edmund Phelps, "The Statistical Theory of Racism and Sexism," *American Economic Review* 62 (September 1972), pp. 659–61; Dennis Aigner and Glen Cain, "Statistical Theories of Discrimination in Labor Markets," *Industrial and Labor Relations Review* 30 (January 1977), pp. 175–87. Roland Fryer and Matthew Jackson, "A Categorical Model of Cognition and Biased Decision Making," *Berkeley Electronic Journal Contributions to Theoretical Economics* 8 (2008), go a step beyond this to analyze the economics of the formation of groups that underlie the statistical theories.

[4] Barbara Bergmann, "The Effect on White Incomes of Discrimination in Employment," *Journal of Political Economy* 79 (March–April 1971), pp. 294–313.

[5] Among the many discussions of this approach, Howard Gardner, *Frames of Mind: The Theory of Multiple Intelligences* (New York: Basic Books, 1983), is perhaps the most well known.

[6] This is a standard Harberger-triangle calculation. Take the extent of wage discrimination against the worst-looking workers as 10 percent as compared to all other workers, and figure their fraction in the workforce is 10 percent. Both of these figures accord with the evidence in chapters 2 and 3, as does the assumption that the ugly are on average as skilled as the rest of the labor force. Then, even if the demand elasticity for the labor of this group of workers is as high as two (see Daniel Hamermesh, *Labor Demand*, Princeton, NJ: Princeton University Press, 1993), the cost to society of misallocating their labor would be about 0.25 percent ($.1 \times .1 \times .5 \times .5$) of total compensation. In 2009, compensation of employees in the United States was about $8 trillion, so that the loss to society of this kind of socially unproductive discrimination is $20 billion.

[7] Markus Möbius and Tanya Rosenblat, "Why Beauty Matters," *American Economic Review* 96 (March 2006), pp. 222–35.

[8] James Andreoni and Ragan Petrie, "Beauty, Gender and Stereotypes: Evidence from Laboratory Experiments," *Journal of Economic Psychology* 29 (2008), pp. 73–93.

[9] Sara Solnick and Maurice Schweitzer, "The Influence of Physical Attractiveness and Gender on Ultimatum Game Decisions," *Organizational Behavior and Human Decision Processes* 79 (September 1999), pp. 199–215.

[10] Michèle Belot, V. Bhaskar, and Jeroen van de Ven, "Beauty and the Sources of Discrimination," unpublished paper, University College–London, 2008. The game show was entitled *Shafted*, and the authors used all episodes from 2002.

[11] "Wimbledon Puts Tennis Babes Front and 'Centre'," http://www.foxnews.com/story/0,2933,529865,00.html.

CHAPTER SEVEN: BEAUTY IN MARKETS FOR FRIENDS, FAMILY, AND FUNDS

[1] See Laurence Iannaconne, "Sacrifice and Stigma: Reducing Free-Riding in Cults, Communes and Other Collectives," *Journal of Political Economy* 100 (April 1992), pp. 271–91.

[2] See Alan Feingold, "Matching for Attractiveness in Romantic Partners and Same-sex Friends: A Meta-Analysis and Theoretical Critique," *Psychological Bulletin* 104 (September 1988), pp. 226–35, for a summary of a large number of studies of this issue.

[3] Marco Castillo, Ragan Petrie, and Maximo Torero, "Beautiful or White? Discrimination in Group Formation," unpublished paper, George Mason University, 2010.

[4] *New York Times*, March 24, 2009, p. D1.

[5] Feingold, "Matching for Attractiveness."

[6] http://news.bbc.co.uk/1/hi/world/asia-pacific/7567239 .stm is among the many websites discussing this statement.

[7] Susan Fisk, "Competition and Social Exchange: Female Attractiveness as an Object of Exchange in Dating Markets," unpublished paper, Department of Sociology, Stanford University, 2008.

[8] Raymond Fisman, Sheena Iyengar, Emir Kamenica, and Itamar Simonson, "Gender Differences in Mate Selection: Evidence from a Speed Dating Experiment," *Quarterly Journal of Economics* 121 (May 2006), pp. 673–97.

[9] Günter Hitsch, Ali Hortaçsu, and Dan Ariely, "Matching and Sorting in Online Dating," *American Economic Review* 100 (2010), pp. 130–63. Hitsch, Hortaçsu, and Ariely, "What Makes You Click?" Mate Preferences and Matching: Outcomes in Online Dating," unpublished paper, University of Chicago, 2006.

[10] For example, the median worker ages 25–34 in 2008 had been at the job for 2.7 years, while the median worker ages 55–64 had been with the same employer for 9.9 years. U.S. Department of Labor, Bureau of Labor Statistics, *Employee Tenure in 2008.*

[11] These estimates are based on regressions that account for spouses' ages, differences in their health, and other characteristics.

[12] Calculated as 10 percent per year times 1.1 (12.4–11.3) years.

[13] Soohyung Lee, "Marriage and Online Mate-Search Services: Evidence from South Korea," unpublished paper, University of Maryland, 2009.

[14] Abhijit Banerjee, Ester Duflo, Maitreesh Ghatak, and Jeanne Lafortune, "Marry for What? Caste and Mate Selection in Modern India," National Bureau of Economic Research, Working Paper No. 14958, 2009.

[15] David Bjerk, "Beauty vs. Earnings: Gender Differences in Earnings and Priorities over Spousal Characteristics in a Match Model," *Journal of Economic Behavior and Organization* 69 (March 2009), pp. 248–59.

[16] See Feingold, "Matching for Attractiveness," which summarizes studies of spouses' looks. David Buss, *The Evolution of Desire: Strategies of Human Mating* (New York: Basic Books, 1994), discusses this more generally.

[17] Liliana Alvarez and Klaus Jaffe, "Narcissism in Mate Selection: Humans Mate Assortatively, as Revealed by Facial Resemblance, Following an Algorithm of 'Self Seeking Like,'" *Evolutionary Psychology* 2 (2004), pp. 177–94.

[18] A test of the entire distribution shows that it is highly nonrandom, with a $X^2(4) = 413.8$, where the 99 percent critical value is 13.28.

[19] http://www.ronsangels.com/index2.html.

[20] On longevity, see Daniel Hamermesh and Frances Hamermesh, "Does Perception of Life Expectancy Reflect Health Knowledge," *American Journal of Public Health* 73 (August 1983), pp. 911–14. The study of the intergenerational relation of heights is the motivation for regression analysis, as Stephen Stigler, *The History of Statistics: The Measurement of Uncertainty Before 1900* (Cambridge, MA: Harvard University Press, 1986), so beautifully discusses. Although there are many other works, I find Leon Kamin, *The Science and Politics of IQ* (New York: Halsted Press, 1974), to be a particularly useful discussion of the issues in the heritability of intelligence.

[21] http://www.breitbart.com/article.php?id=CNG.33f98480 869b474b6d10cafcf0b1de64.7c1&show_article=1.

[22] http://snltranscripts.jt.org/84/84iwhitelikeeddie.phtml.

[23] Alicia Munnell, Geoffrey Tootle, Lynn Browne, and James McEneany, "Mortgage Lending in Boston: Interpreting HMDA Data," *American Economic Review* 86 (March 1996), pp. 25–53.

[24] Enrichetta Ravina, "Love and Loans: The Effect of Beauty and Personal Characteristics in Credit Markets," unpublished paper, New York University, March 2008; Jefferson Duarte, Stephan Siegel, and Lance Young, "Trust and Credit," unpublished paper, Rice University, November 2008. Devin Pope and Justin Sydnor, "What's in a Picture? Evidence of Discrimination from Prosper.com," unpublished paper, Wharton School, University of Pennsylvania, 2008.

CHAPTER EIGHT: LEGAL PROTECTION FOR THE UGLY

[1] http://www.sfgov.org/site/sfhumanrights_index.asp?id= 4583.

[2] See Deborah Rhode, *The Beauty Bias: The Injustice of Appearance in Life and Law* (New York: Oxford University Press, 2010), chapter 6, for a longer discussion of these provisions.

[3] Discussion of the California Fair Employment and Housing Act, California Department of Consumer Affairs, is at (http://www.dca.ca.gov/publications/landlordbook/discrimination.shtml).

[4] http://wallis.kezenfogva.iif.hu/eu_konyvtar/projektek/vocational_rehabilitiation/france/fra_rap/leg.htm.

[5] For a discussion of the cases here, as well as many others, see Jennifer Fowler-Hermes, "Beauty and the Beast in the Workplace: Appearance-based Discrimination under EEO Laws," *Florida Bar Journal* 75 (April 2001).

[6] The cases discussed here and the legal issues generally are presented by Elizabeth Theran, "Legal Theory on Weight Discrimination," in *Weight Bias: Nature, Consequences and Remedies*, ed. Kelly Brownell, Rebecca Puhl, Leslie Rudd, and Marlene Schwartz (New York: Guilford Press, 2005), pp. 195–211.

[7] James McDonald, "Civil Rights for the Aesthetically-Challenged," *Employee Relations Law Journal* 29 (Autumn 2003), pp. 118–29, discusses the development of law in this area.

[8] Timothy Van Dyck, Edwards, Engell, Palmer & Dodge, July 17, 2008, http://www.employmentlawalliance.com/en/node/2393.

[9] The case of the Malone twins, Boston firefighters whose claim to be African American on their job applications was eventually challenged, is the most well-known example of the difficulties in classification and with self-classification (*New York Times*, October 9, 1988; http://www.nytimes.com/1988/10/09/us/boston-case-raises-questions-on-misuse-of-affirmative-action.html?pagewanted=all). Other cases have arisen. In Washington State, when individuals who had listed themselves as being members of various protected racial/ethnic groups were asked to provide some supporting evidence, 3 percent switched their self-description to Caucasian (http://aad.english.ucsb.edu/docs/proof.html).

[10] http://www.eeoc.gov/stats/charges.html.

[11] See, for example, http://www.radiancemagazine.com/kids_project/body_image.html.

[12] For a discussion of these events, see http://www.dallasnews.com/sharedcontent/dws/fea/lifetravel/stories/082708dnmetabercrombie.4027698.html.

[13] Calculations are by the author from the Current Population Survey, Merged Outgoing Rotation Groups, 2008.

[14] Ibid. Calculations using data for 2008 based on the usual earnings of men with the same education, age, hours of work, location, and marital status.

[15] Judith Hellerstein, David Neumark, and Kenneth Troske, "Wages, Productivity, and Worker Characteristics: Evidence from Plant-Level Production Functions and Wage Equations," *Journal of Labor Economics* 17 (July 1999), pp. 409–46; and John Haltiwanger, Julia Lane, and James Spletzer, "Wages, Productivity, and the Dynamic Interaction of Businesses and Workers," *Labour Economics* 14 (June 2007), pp. 575–602.

[16] For a discussion of the very low, but rising intermarriage rates in the United States, see Roland Fryer, "Guess Who's Been Coming to Dinner? Trends in Interracial Marriage over the 20th Century," *Journal of Economic Perspectives* 21 (Spring 2007), pp. 71–90. In 2008, 21 percent of African Americans had not completed high school, while only 12 percent of non-Hispanic whites had that little education. Only 17 percent of African Americans had at least graduated from college or university, while 29 percent of non-Hispanic whites had done so. Computed using the same methods and data as provided in note 13.

[17] See Clark Nardinelli and Curtis Simon, "Customer Racial Discrimination in the Market for Memorabilia: The Case of Baseball," *Quarterly Journal of Economics* 105 (August 1990), pp. 575–95; Orley Ashenfelter and Timothy Hannan, "Sex Discrimination and Product Market Competition: The Case of the Banking Industry," *Quarterly Journal of Economics* 101 (February 1986), pp. 149–73.

[18] Computed using the same methods and data as provided in note 13.

[19] See Hellerstein et al., "Wages, Productivity, and Worker Characteristics," and Haltiwanger et al., "Wages, Productivity, and the Dynamic Interaction of Businesses and Workers."

[20] Rhode, *The Beauty Bias*.

[21] An early study of this issue is George Borjas, "The Substitutability of Black, Hispanic and White Labor," *Economic Inquiry* 21 (January 1983), pp. 93–106. See also most of the studies in Daniel Hamermesh and Frank Bean, eds., *Help or Hindrance: The Economic Implications of Immigration for African-Americans* (New York: Russell Sage Foundation, 1998), particularly those by George Johnson and by Borjas.

CHAPTER NINE: PROSPECTS FOR THE LOOKS-CHALLENGED

[1]   . . . he fluttered pulses when he said,
     "Good-morning," and he glittered when he walked
     . . .
     And Richard Cory, one calm summer night,
     Went home and put a bullet in his head.

Edwin Arlington Robinson

[2] Calculations from the 1971 and 1978 Quality of American Life surveys. The only scholarly study that seems to have examined this issue using a nationally representative sample employed the 1978 data to summarize a happiness measure in each of the five categories of beauty: Debra Umberson and Michael Hughes, "The Impact of Physical Attractiveness on Achievement and Psychological Well-Being," *Social Psychology Quarterly* 50 (September 1987), pp. 227–36. See also Daniel Hamermesh and Jason Abrevaya, "'Beauty Is the Promise of Happiness'?", IZA Discussion Paper No. 5600, 2011.

[3] Calculations from the same sources as in note 2.

[4] Anthony Synott, sociologist, quoted in *International Herald-Tribune*, November 4, 2008.

[5] S. Michael Kalick, Leslie Zebrowitz, Judity Langlois, and Robert Johnson, "Does Human Facial Attractiveness Honestly Advertise Health?" *Psychological Science* 9 (January 1998), pp. 8–13.

[6] Lisa DeBruine, Benedict Jones, John Crawford, Lisa Welling, and Anthony Little, "The Health of a Nation Predicts Their Mate Preferences: Cross-cultural Variation in Women's Preferences for Masculinized Male Faces," *Proceedings of the Royal Society, Part B*, 277 (August 2010), pp. 2405–10.

[7] The idea goes back at least to Richard Nelson, "A Theory of the Low-Level Equilibrium Trap in Underdeveloped Economies," *American Economic Review* 46 (December 1956), pp. 894–908. John Dagsvik and Boyan Jovanovic, "Was the Great Depression a Low-Level Equilibrium?" *European Economic Review* 38 (December 1994), pp. 1711–29, discuss it in the context of macroeconomics.

[8] Gary Becker and Kevin Murphy, "A Theory of Rational Addiction," *Journal of Political Economy* 96 (August 1988), pp. 675–700, is the lead study expounding this idea. The application to cigarettes is by Gary Becker, Michael Grossman, and Kevin Murphy, "An Empirical Analysis of Cigarette Addiction," *American Economic Review* 84 (June 1994), pp. 396–418.

[9] *More*, October 2008, p. 143.

INDEX

Abercrombie and Fitch, 159
actors, 13–15, 32, 67–71, 110, 176, 179
advertising, 88–93, 96, 139, 142–43,
    146, 191n8
aesthetics, 12
affirmative action, 151–52, 199n9
African Americans, 144; affirmative ac-
    tion and, 151–52, 199n9; education
    and, 200n16; employment and,
    58–59, 76, 108, 110; legal issues and,
    154, 157, 161–62, 165; Malone
    twins and, 199n9; standards of
    beauty and, 29–30
age: Age Discrimination in Employment
    Act (ADEA) and, 150; Americans
    with Disabilities Act (ADA) and,
    150–51, 155, 158, 167–69; attorneys
    and, 60–63; dating and, 133; earn-
    ings and, 44, 52, 56, 59–63, 75–79,
    83, 118, 190n21; employment and,
    44, 52, 56, 59–63, 75–79, 83, 118,
    190n21; group formation and, 129;
    legal protection and, 148, 150, 153;
    prostitutes and, 75; standards of
    beauty and, 11, 22–23, 27–34; van-
    ity and, 3–4

Age Discrimination in Employment Act
    (ADEA), 150
American Economic Association, 81–82
Americans with Disabilities Act (ADA),
    150–51, 155, 158, 167–69
analysis of variance (ANOVA),
    183nn9,11
Arden, Dale, 176
artistic ability, 103, 110, 176
Asian Americans, 15–16, 29
assisted living facilities, 4
athletics, 66, 82–83, 120, 127–30, 179
attorneys, 188n4; administrative, 71;
    age effects and, 60–63; compensat-
    ing beauty-damaged worker and,
    63–64; corporate, 71; employment
    and, 48–52, 60–64, 67–68, 71–72,
    78–79, 83, 88, 91, 102, 119–20;
    financial, 71; *L.A. Law* and, 68–71;
    Law School Aptitude Test (LSAT)
    and, 52; legal issues and, 157, 159
    (*see also* legal issues); litigators, 68;
    lookism and, 102, 119–21; produc-
    tive beauty and, 102, 119–20; regu-
    lation, 71; tax, 68
Australia, 15, 49, 76, 82, 133

social issues (*cont.*)

    also discrimination); education and, 43, 46, 63, 73, 90, 127, 132–39, 151, 160–62, 199n14, 200n16; Equal Employment Opportunity Commission (EEOC) and, 150, 155, 158; Equal Pay Act (EPA) and, 150; Executive Order 10925 and, 151; Executive Order 11246 and, 151; fairness and, 148–49; group formation and, 125–26, 128–30, 146; legal protection for the ugly and, 148–69; market for beautiful children and, 141–44; marriage and, 126 (*see also* marriage); politicians and, 15–17, 75, 78; positive strategies for, 177–80; religion and, 106, 130, 150, 153–54, 167

socially productive beauty, 103, 108–11

social networks, 49, 133

social skills, 108, 142

specific occupations: actors, 13–15, 32, 67–71, 176, 179; athletes, 82–83; attorneys, 48–52, 60–64, 67–68, 71–72, 78–79, 83, 88, 91, 102, 119–20, 159, 188n4; choosing, 66–72, 84; criminals, 83–84; economists, 81–82; opera singers, 66, 71, 187n1; politicians, 15, 17, 67, 75–78; preference and, 68, 84; professors, 24, 26, 29, 67, 79–84, 106, 120–21; prostitutes, 9, 67, 73–75, 78, 91, 109; radio broadcasters, 66–67, 84; requirements and, 67–68; salespeople, 67, 88, 91, 106, 109; size of beauty effects and, 72–84; skills and, 71, 84; sorting by beauty and, 84–85

speed-dating, 134–35

sperm donors, 141, 144

spokespersons, 88, 120

standards of beauty, 10; age and, 11, 22–23, 27–34; agreement on, 11–13, 15,

18–21, 24–28, 31–32, 35–36, 99, 126, 156–57; behavior and, 13, 18, 21, 36; body weight/height and, 53–54; cultural differences and, 4, 16, 21, 23, 26–27, 30–31; definitions of beauty and, 11–17; executives and, 7, 62, 68, 78, 89–99; faces and, 12–15, 19–20, 31, 33, 35, 53–54, 61–62, 66–67, 82–84, 98–99, 112–14, 142, 155, 167, 175–76; future changes in, 173–80; gender and, 28–32, 36; importance of, 18–19; increasing beauty and, 32–35; marriage and, 18; measurement for, 19 (*see also* scale of beauty); men and, 13–15, 18, 22–30; race and, 28–32; ugliness and, 23–24, 28, 31–32, 36; United States and, 15–16, 23, 27, 30, 32; universal, 15–16, 21, 27; women and, 13–15, 18, 22–25, 28–30, 34, 36

start-up companies, 87

statistics: age and, 183n12; analysis of variance (ANOVA) and, 183nn9,11; chi-square, 183n10; Harberger-triangle calculation and, 193n6; employment and, 45, 47, 76–77, 81, 99, 106–8, 117; loans and, 145; marriage and, 137; multivariate regression and, 185n1, 196n11, 197n20; standards of beauty and, 24, 27

stereotypes, 30, 106–7

strength, 84, 103, 131, 137

success: beautiful children and, 142; dating and, 131, 134–35; dressing for, 33; education and, 131; employment and, 48, 60, 67–68, 71–81, 84, 87–88, 91, 98, 100; legal issues and, 155, 160; obtaining credit and, 145; productive beauty and, 109, 119; reproductive, 131, 142, 175; standards of beauty and, 13, 31, 33

"Summertime" (opera aria), 139